For EVERY MOUNTAIN

MOUNTAIN

Learning to THRIVE While in the Valley

Ramona Y. Simmons

FOR EVERY MOUNTAIN

Learning to THRIVE While in the Valley

Copyright © 2018 by Pastor G Ministries

All Scripture quotations unless otherwise indicated are taken from The Holy Bible, English Standard Version.

Simmons, Ramona Y., 1974-

Senior Editor: Jamila M. Woodard

Edited by: Dr. Lisa Jack

Cover design: Paula McDade

Author photo: Omar Lampley

Library of Congress Cataloging-in-Publication Data

ISBN 978-0692122242

2018939283

First Printing 2018

Printed in the United States of America

The LORD will fulfill his purpose for me; your steadfast love, O LORD, endures forever. Do not forsake the work of your hands.

Psalm 138:8

In memory of my daddy, Charles McKinley Simmons, my earthly example of God's unconditional love. Your deposit in my life made a huge difference.

To my four children, Khalil (Bubba), Rachael (Doodlebug), LaBraia (Peaches), and Raven (Princess) may this book serve as a reminder throughout your life of the faithfulness of God.

To the earthly shepherds God has blessed me with who helped grow my love for God's Word and challenged me to follow God in all things I salute you.

The late Pastor H. A. Walker
True Vine Baptist Church

The late Pastor A. Glenn Woodberry
Greater Mount Olive Baptist Church

Pastor Teron V. Gaddis
Greater Bethel Baptist Church

Finally, to my team and my sister/friends
Your prayers, encouragement and support
meant more than any edit or rewrite through this
process. You have walked through this journey
with me reminding me that I could do it because
God said I could. I love you all more than you
will ever know. This is a WIN for all of us.

Ordinary People
James Cleveland

Ordinary People

God uses plain old ordinary people.

He uses people just like you and me who are
willing to do as He commands.

He uses people that will give their all. No
matter how small your all may seem to you.

Little becomes much when you place it in the
Master's Hands.

Table of Contents

FOREWORD
PASTOR TERON V. GADDIS

My grandmother taught me a very valuable lesson as a young college student. One of my favorite things was standing in her kitchen as she taught me how to cook and bake. One weekend I was complaining and crying about how "everything' was going wrong. She never commented or chimed in she just kept on pulling ingredients from the refrigerator and cabinets. Then as only should could she asked, "Son, are you hungry and would you like a snack?" I quickly answer, "Yes, mother I would love something to eat." She said, "here have some cooking oil." To which I answered, "no ma'am." She then offered me a couple of raw eggs, a cup of flour, a few tablespoons of baking powder. This went on for a few minutes until she said, "of course you would not want these items separately because by themselves they would not taste good. But when they are put together in the right way, using the right measurements, cooked in the right temperature, they make a wonderful delicious cake. She went on to explain how God take the mountains and the valleys of life and turn them into something good for us.

For all of us life is a series of mountains and valleys. Each moment and each morning bring something different. One moment life and living will at time be blissful, beautiful, bountiful, blooming and blossoming with blessings and then without warning turn to messy, ugly, dirty, shimmy, yucky, vicious, vile, violent, hard, harsh and heavy.

In this life, we must deal with both...

- Bright and black days
- Delightful and distressing days
- Terrific and troubling days
- Glorious and gloomy days

- Peaceful and painful days and
- Happy and hurtful days.

However, here's some good news. No matter what the day brings, we can be sure God is always at work. We will all come to a point in our pilgrimage on this planet where we will not know what to do. I want to remind you that you can always trust God is working for you, through you and in you.

I want to submit to you; valley lows and mountain tops are only a route to a closer walk with God. There are no alternate routes, no alternatives ways or no rerouting when it comes to preparing us for His plan, His purpose and His promise. When the Pharaoh finally recognized the powerful hand of God and let the Israelites go he later sent the Egyptian army to chase the Israelites. There was an angry army behind them, mountains on both sides and the Red Sea in front.

There was no way for them to go around it. But God made a way for them to cross. No matter what you may be up against, mountains or valleys, we must always remember God will make a way. Remember His grace, His leading, His mercy, His care and His love will never, ever fail. We may not always agree or see how, what or why God is doing what He is doing. In other words, He may do the opposite of what we expect and anticipate Him to do.

I know this because I have been guilty of moaning, complaining and crying. Why would God allow this or that? Asking why me rather than why not me? Whenever that happens I have discovered I failed to do what God has asked me to do. In other words, I stopped being the created and started trying to be the creator. I stopped being the son and started trying to be the Father. As we journey through valleys and mountains, we sometimes tend to question God's hand when we should be trusting God's heart. He knows what we need better than we do.

After 35 years of ministry and 25 years of leading the Greater Bethel Church of Oklahoma City, I have ministered and celebrated with those whom I serve as undershepherd and walk with them through the good and the bad times, time of baptism, times of celebrating life and times of burials.

I have had the great opportunity to know Ramona Y. Simmons for over 20 years and have the privilege to be her pastor. She serves as my executive pastoral assistant for the past 6 years. She is an incredible mother to her children and an anointed teacher and writer. I believe her transparency will truly bless those who are faced with disappointment, discouragement, despair, depression, divorce and death both for the believer and unbeliever. The eight principles are imperative for those who live in the real world and understand that mountains and valleys are permitted in our lives to strengthen our outward conduct, our inward character and our upward commitment.

This simple but powerful and compelling book walks you through the life of a real person, dealing with real problems in the real world and how trusting in God's power, presences and promises will transform and strengthen your life.

As you read this book it is my prayer that, "Every valley shall be filled, and every mountain and hill shall be made low, and the crooked shall become straight, and the rough places shall become level ways, and all flesh shall see the salvation of God," Luke 3:5-6 (ESV).

Mother to Son

BY LANGSTON HUGHES

Well, son, I'll tell you:
Life for me ain't been no crystal stair.
It's had tacks in it,
And splinters,
And boards torn up,
And places with no carpet on the floor—
Bare.
But all the time
I'se been a-climbin' on,
And reachin' landin's,
And turnin' corners,
And sometimes goin' in the dark
Where there ain't been no light.
So boy, don't you turn back.
Don't you set down on the steps
'Cause you finds it's kinder hard.
Don't you fall now—
For I'se still goin', honey,
I'se still climbin',
And life for me ain't been no crystal stair.

OPEN LETTER

I have a confession. I lived over half of my life mad at God. There I said it. God had been unfair to me and I did not deserve all the hell He was taking me through. I was a pretty good child. I always tried to do what was required of me. I made good grades. My parents very rarely had to discipline me. I started very early in life trying to make sure everyone around me was happy. Yes. I was the typical people pleaser. I never wanted anyone to be mad at me and so I sacrificed my own needs and desires trying to live up to the expectations of everyone around me. What I didn't realize was I was setting myself up for a huge let down. I did not realize that there was only One individual I needed to please and the benefits to serving Him were far greater than anything I could ever imagine.

There was never a time I didn't know church. I grew up in church. In fact, I was one of the ones who could say I was at church almost seven days a week. I accepted Jesus Christ as my Lord and Savior at the age of twelve attending True Vine Independent Church in Spencer, Oklahoma where the late Reverend Herman A. Walker was my Pastor. I was taught to be an active church member as a child; carrying that practice into my adulthood. Church was no different than any other area of my life. I wanted to please my Pastor and my Sunday School teacher and even God, or so I thought. Hey, at least I was doing all the right things. This is why when life began to take a turn for the worse I just didn't understand. Beginning with my parents divorcing and then me moving out of my parents' home at fourteen to live with my Godmother and her family. Followed by getting pregnant in college, dropping out, two suicide attempts, two failed marriages, physical, verbal, and mental abuse and a lifelong battle with depression and anxiety.

I have always been told God loves me and He wants what is best for me. Reread the paragraph above and tell me if that sound like something someone would give to someone they love. Those are things I wouldn't even give to my enemies. Yet God, who is Omniscient, Omnipresent, and Omnipotent decided to give those things to me as a part of my life story.

Here is the kicker. For the most part most of the people in my life who are close to me don't know any of this. Remember I said I was a people pleaser. My job was to smile and encourage others. I had perfected the mask that I wore. Like the Secret deodorant commercial slogan, "Never let them see you sweat." And I was that one. I continued my routine. I smiled when the cameras were on and then went home to my bed of depression with tears and no will to live.

I was a good Christian too. I diligently read and studied my Bible. I had a pretty good prayer life. (the one all my friends and family called on to pray for them when they were in a jam.) I attended church all the time. Taught Sunday School and Women's Bible Study. A leader in the Women's Ministry at my church and in the District Association in the state where I lived. Sang in the choir, wrote an encouraging blog, and spoke at conferences.

From the outside looking in I had a pretty good life. I got married and divorced and married again. I once had a girlfriend tell me, "You never have to be alone. You can always get a man." What she did not know was that yes, I was married but I was also very alone.

As you are reading I know you are wondering why am I sharing all this? Two reasons: first reason is because through all my heartbreak and heartache, disappointment with myself and with others I learned that God had a purpose for all my pain. Second reason is the reason you are reading this book. There are many like me who have suffered great hurt and pain and have directed their anger at God instead of understanding that the day you were born God set into motion a great journey of trust designed solely to bring Him glory.

This life we live is not about us. My current Pastor, Reverend Teron V. Gaddis of the Greater Bethel Church, Oklahoma City, Oklahoma, said something so very profound one Wednesday evening at Bible Study. His statement was "God doesn't need us for the saving process, yet He chooses to use us to help bring others to Him only to later reward us in eternity for something He never needed us for to begin with. Now that's love."

God has a purpose and a plan for every one of us. The Word says in **Jeremiah 29:11**, "For I know the plans that I have for you, plans to prosper and not to harm you..." While we may not understand His process, we must trust His heart for His children. As you read through the pages of this book I want you to keep that in mind. There is absolutely nothing that has happened in your life that has not been a part of God's plan.

My late Pastor A. Glenn Woodberry of the Greater Mount Olive Baptist Church in Oklahoma City, Oklahoma said, "God cannot use you greatly until He has bruised you deeply." Over thirty years ago I gave God control of my life. At twelve I really didn't understand what that meant. Today I do.

Contrary to what you may have heard or even been taught this life is not just about getting to the mountaintop. Mountaintops are rare. We spend most of our lives down in the valley. The key to life is learning how to live in the valley by trusting God. So, what does that look like? This process is different for everyone. However, there are some key principles I want to share with you that I pray will bless your life. Principles I pray will help you to continue living your life for the glory and honor of God.

Before we dive in I want to share one of my favorite verses in the Bible. I discovered this verse when I realized my first marriage was failing. Hardly a day goes by that I don't quote this verse.

II Corinthians 4:16-18 says, 16 So we do not lose heart. Though our outer self is wasting away, our inner self is being renewed day by day. 17 For this light momentary affliction is preparing for us an eternal weight of glory beyond all comparison, 18 as we look not to the things that are seen but to the things that are unseen. For the things that are seen are transient, but the things that are unseen are eternal.

Principle #1

Valley lows do not discriminate.

There is an unfortunate mistake many Christians make. We see our salvation as the ticket to problem-free living. We understand we may have some problems but nothing too major. After all, we're saved now. We surrendered, gave God our heart and the preacher our hand. The time has come for smooth sailing.

Let me share with you the problem with this line of thinking. It contradicts the Bible.

John 16:33 says, *"I have said these things to you, that in me you may have peace. In the world you will have tribulation. But take heart; I have overcome the world."*

James 1:2-4 says, *"Count it all joy, my brothers, when you meet trials of various kinds, 3 for you know that the testing of your faith produces steadfastness. 4 And let steadfastness*

have its full effect, that you may be perfect and complete, lacking in nothing."

1 Peter 5:10 says, "And after you have suffered a little while, the God of all grace, who has called you to his eternal glory in Christ, will himself restore, confirm, strengthen, and establish you."

These are just a few verses that prove the error of this theory. There are many more. My summation of these verses is simple. Life will consist of both mountaintops and valley lows. No one is exempt.

One of the best examples I can give you is Job. It begins this way.

"There was a man in the land of Uz whose name was Job, and that man was blameless and upright, one who feared God and turned away from evil. Job 1:1

Twelve verses later we read these words.

Now there was a day when his sons and daughters were eating and drinking wine in their oldest brother's house, 14 and there came a messenger to Job and said, "The oxen were plowing and the donkeys feeding beside them, 15 and the Sabeans fell upon them and took them and struck down the servants with the edge of the sword, and I alone have escaped to tell you." 16 While he was yet speaking, there came another and said, "The fire of God fell from heaven and burned up the sheep and the servants and consumed them, and I alone have escaped to tell you." 17 While he was yet speaking, there came another and said, "The Chaldeans formed three groups and made a raid on the camels and took them and struck down the servants with the edge of the sword, and I alone have escaped to tell you." 18 While he was yet speaking, there came another and said, "Your sons and daughters were eating and drinking wine in their oldest brother's house,

19 and behold, a great wind came across the wilderness and struck the four corners of the house, and it fell upon the young people, and they are dead, and I alone have escaped to tell you."

Verse 1 = Mountaintop

Verses 13-19 = Valley

Now before I go any further I must make this observation. These things happened to Job. Job who was described as 'blameless and upright, one who feared God and turned away from evil'. Notice Job did not say these things about Himself, God said these things about Him. Many of us live mediocre lives in service to God and yet we expect to never go through anything. We should probably expect to go through some things because we know we are not right. We have given God some of us, but not all of us. We give God some of our time, but not all our time. We have turned away from some evil, but there is still that one thing we just cannot give up. There I said it. Okay now on with the lesson.

What does the story of Job teach us about our Christian walk?

You cannot live good enough to escape trouble.

The very first thing we are told about Job is his character.   What do the words upright and blameless mean? Something upright is vertically erect or evenly distributed. It speaks of a person who is genuine and forthright. A person who is upright is unchanging in his or her standards. In most cases this characteristic is most fitting for our holy God. It was Moses who described Him this way in **Deuteronomy 32:4**. *"He is the Rock, his works are perfect, and all his ways are just. A faithful God who does no wrong, upright and just is he."* In those days when there were many idol gods, this was unheard of. Yet this was the

God who had shown Himself over and over to the children of Israel. And here we find this term used to describe the character of Job.

Job did more than do what was right. He had integrity of heart. Honesty and goodness were at the center of his being. His uprightness was not situational. No matter what he had to face in life, Job always did what was right in the eyes of God.

Job was also blameless. People could not accuse him of wrongdoing and neither did God. In the Old Testament this concept is usually connected to animals that were sacrificed. Only animals that were without blemish could be sacrificed. It was a violation of biblical law if blemished animals were sacrificed.

In the New Testament the word blameless was associated with Jesus Christ who, through his work on the cross, became our perfect sacrifice who was without blemish. It is God's intention that we, as Christians, obtain a position of blamelessness. **Ephesians 1:4** It is the hope of Christ that one day He will be able to present the church to Himself without spot or wrinkle. **Ephesians 5:27**

Being blameless is about position. It is a benefit. When we accept Jesus Christ as our personal Savior, blamelessness is imputed to us through the death and resurrection. We are protected until the day of judgment. God is the only one who has the right to accuse and condemn us. But thanks be to God for grace whereby He chooses not to; but instead declares us not guilty.

Salvation is not a free ticket to sin until Jesus returns.

There is yet another way to look at the word blameless. This is more about us and how we choose to live. Salvation is not a free ticket to sin until Jesus returns. Instead our salvation should cause us to say we owe God everything and want to live in a way that pleases Him. It is the outward reputation that comes from our inward moral character. Every Christian should make every effort to live a life that reflects the One who saved us. We should desire to make God proud.

In 2011 my dad was diagnosed with stage 4 cancer. He was given six months to live. My dad was 70 years old when he received his diagnosis. The news came as a shock to all eight of his children because at 70 my dad was still doing everything. He was cutting grass, working on cars, attending all his grandchildren's' events, and taking pretty good care of himself.

My dad had lived a pretty blessed life. He had never been hospitalized and never really been sick except for a cold here or there. So, when the diagnosis came he told his children he would not undergo any treatment and was ready to meet His Savior. We were very saddened by the news. However, after praying and spending a few days in the hospital he had a change of heart and decided to undergo treatment and spend this time loving on his children and grandchildren even more.

After over a month in the hospital my dad came to live with me. It was then I had the opportunity to see who my dad had become. My dad was not perfect, but he was close. I saw him praying. I saw him reading His Bible. In fact, one of my most cherished possession I now have is his Bible. He had literally highlighted and marked up every page of that Bible. He would go to his chemotherapy treatments on Mondays and get out on Wednesdays. And on Wednesday nights he was sitting next to me in Bible Study. My daddy was my pew partner.

Teaching the Bible has always been a joy. And on the day my dad walked in and took a seat in my class, I became an even better student of the Bible; wanting to make him proud of me, aware there were things I had done to disappoint him in the past. This was a new opportunity given to me for making right some of that disappointment. One of my greatest joys was hearing him say to me that I taught him something one Sunday afternoon after class. I don't know if he was just saying that or if I really did. All I know is it made me feel good.

In the same way I wanted my earthly father to be proud of me, we all should want our Heavenly Father to be proud of us. We will never teach God anything. He should be able to observe our spiritual growth during our journey that makes Him proud that we are His children.

Here we have Job who has been attributed the same characteristics attributed to God and yet we find him living verses 13-19. I am sure Job did not live that way thinking he would escape trouble. He lived to please God. Many of us believe that God keeps track of how good we are and the good deeds we do to determine not only if we will have to go through tests and trials, but also the severity of our tests and trials.

God doesn't operate that way. The reason for tests and trials and trouble in our lives is to make us into the image of His Son. Holiness not happiness. Salvation did not do that. Salvation set us on the right path. Before salvation we were on the wrong road, headed in the wrong direction. It does not matter how much success you might have achieved before Christ, until God found you and you accepted His call you were on the wrong path.

It is like a person who is driving to a new destination. More than likely the use of a map or GPS is necessary otherwise the individual will drive around aimlessly. For those married women who may be reading this, you probably relate this to being in the car when your husband is driving. For some reason men are too stubborn often, to stop and ask for directions. They believe there is something in their DNA that automatically tells them how to get everywhere.

I am grateful for the feature in the GPS system that allows for rerouting. We may miss an exit and it will reroute us to the next closest exit giving us another chance to get off and continue the right path. Of course, this means it will take us longer to get to our destination. However, it does not mean we will not arrive.

I have a question for you. When will you begin to thank God for your tests and trials? Will you ever acknowledge the benefit before the blessing? How many times will you have to be rerouted because you get off the path when trouble comes? When will God finally be able to say about you what He said about Job? *"...and that man was blameless and upright, one who feared God and turned away from evil.* **Job 1:1**

Righteous living does not exempt you from trouble. Abundant living is not devoid of trials. Our goal should be to make our Heavenly Father proud by staying the course even amid trials. As we walk through this journey of trust we must remember that we are never alone. The test come after the lesson not before. What qualified Job for this test was he had already gone through some things that made God call him blameless and upright.

Abundant living is not devoid of trials.

Remember what James 1:2-4 says, *"Count it all joy, my brothers, when you meet trials of various kinds, [3] for you know that the testing of your faith produces steadfastness. [4] And let steadfastness have its full effect, that you may be perfect and complete, lacking in nothing.*

Principle #2

Valley living prepares you for the mountaintop.

I will begin where I left off in Principle 1 with **James 1:2-4**.

[2] *"Count it all joy, my brothers, when you meet trials of various kinds, [3] for you know that the testing of your faith produces steadfastness. [4] And let steadfastness have its full effect, that you may be perfect and complete, lacking in nothing."*

As a mother one thing I have become better at is cooking. I have four children with very critical taste buds and they want flavorful food. One of their favorite dishes is chicken spaghetti. They believe that the chicken spaghetti just magically appears because most of the time when I cook it I do it after they have gone to sleep. Two reasons for this. The first is because it is a long process and the second reason is that I like to cook and spend time with God.

The first step in the process is that I bake my chicken. Most recipes for chicken spaghetti tell you to boil the chicken. I bake my chicken because the flavor of the chicken is just better with all the seasonings and the bell peppers and onions that surround it. While the chicken is baking I dice my green, red, and yellow bell peppers. I also cut up my cheese and place all these items in the refrigerator.

After this I began making my homemade chicken broth which is another step I changed from the original recipe. Once the seasonings have marinated in the broth and come to a boil, I add my spaghetti noodles. Right about this time it is time for the chicken to come out of the oven. I let it cook for a minute and then I shred the chicken.

Now comes the easy part, mixing everything together. I pull out a large dutch oven pot and I add the spaghetti noodles, bell peppers, cheese, cream of chicken, cream of mushroom, stewed tomatoes, some of the chicken broth and lastly the shredded chicken. I stir it all together by hand, cover the pot and place it in the oven on 375. After baking for about twenty minutes I take the pot out of the oven and add a shredded cheese blend to the top. And if I am feeling extra nice I cook some bacon, cut it up and sprinkle it on top. I place it back in the oven for about seven minutes and voila, chicken spaghetti.

For a dish that my children love and request regularly, they have no idea the time and preparation it takes to make the dish just right. Now I could take a few shortcuts that wouldn't necessarily hurt the dish, it just doesn't taste as good. I could boil the chicken. I could even purchase a rotisserie chicken from Sam's. I could use store bought chicken broth. I could even omit a few of the canned ingredients. It just would not taste the same. For the desired result to be achieved preparation and the right ingredients are necessary.

In this first chapter of James, he tells us what the key ingredients are for a Christian to receive God's divine result of glorification. In verse 2 we are told to ***count*** it ***all joy*** when we ***meet*** trials of ***various*** kinds... I want you to pay close attention to the words that I have underlined.

The first word I have underlined is "count". The KJV tells us to *consider it all joy.* To count means to think, to regard, to consider or to deliberate. Notice here James does not tell us to be happy. He tells us to take everything into consideration. When a jury goes back to deliberate during a trial they are given clear and concise instructions. The jury is instructed to consider the facts and bring back a verdict. Here James is telling us to consider the source, consider the purpose, and reach a verdict. Will tests and trials achieve the desired result?

God is telling us to think, regard, consider it ALL JOY! This is not a mixed joy or a temporary joy. Not some joy with the mixture of grief. Not some joy with much complaining along the way. It is a joy that encompasses the entire length, depth, and width of the trial.

I live in Oklahoma where we experience tornadoes. The severity of a tornado can range from an F0 to an F5. These categories are based upon the estimated maximum winds occurring within the funnel. Depending on the expected severity of the tornado, the meteorologist will give specific instructions for your safety and survival. Whenever there is a storm headed our way it is usually predicted several days in advance. This allows the residents to prepare. The day the storm arrives sometimes they are right in their predictions and other times they are wrong and the storm is not as severe. Regardless, it is still always important to prepare. Some storms in our lives will be minor and some will be major. However, a Christian should never be surprised. Storms will come. Tests will come. Trials will come. Trouble will come. I did not underline the word *when* in verse 2. However, it is important to note the writer says when not if. When…meaning not maybe, but definitely. When… not if.

God has made the soul capable of growth and enlargement. The soul experiences growth and enlargement through tests and trials allowed by God. We must never forget the trial experienced by Job was not a standalone decision by the enemy. The enemy had to get God's permission. Then and only then could the trial begin. And so, if God allowed it then the purpose was greater than to make Job sad or angry or even because of some sin, as Job's friends implied.

I want to ask you to do something for me. Stop reading and take out a piece of paper. Write down the last trial God allowed in your life that you survived. Underneath that make two columns. In the left column I want you to list the things you lost. On the right column I want you to list the things you gained.

Earlier today I was having a conversation with my best friend. I was reflecting on a very difficult time in my life. I talked about the things I lost and at the time I thought I could not make it without them. Through the situation I learned I could. In fact, I learned what I gained far outweighed what I had. After years of talking about and teaching the Word of God, I finally had more than book knowledge, I had heart knowledge. My reference for the God I spoke about was my own life. I no longer had to guess that God was a Healer because He healed my broken heart. I no longer had to guess if God was a Provider because when I had no job, He took care of me. I no longer had to guess if God was a Mind-Regulator because when I had a nervous breakdown He steadied my mind. I no longer had to guess if God was a Friend to the friendless until some of who I thought were my very best friends walked away from me.

One thing we must never lose sight of is God's desire for His children is holiness not happiness. It is not about our comfort. If we acknowledge God to be God, we must also acknowledge He knows what is best. It means His knowledge supersedes what we think about ourselves. In these verses in the book of James he tells of one characteristic that is critical to our holiness. The characteristic is steadfastness.

Steadfastness means having the ability to patiently endure. One who is steadfast is not wishy washy. A steadfast person is confident in what He knows and no matter what may arise contrary to what He knows, He remains confident in the truth. To be steadfast means you are firmly fixed in your faith. Paul said it this way in **Romans 5:3-5**, *"Not only that, but we rejoice in our sufferings, knowing that suffering produces endurance, and endurance produces character, and character produces hope, and hope does not put us to shame, because God's love has been poured into our hearts through the Holy Spirit who has been given to us."*

When your faith is tried the goal is improvement not failure. As we train in the school of affliction God desires for us to become more and more patient under trial. Through our trials God reveals Himself to us. As we come to understand more about the heart of God our faith should grow. This means that we are not running to God praying Lord get me out of this every time we face a trial. Instead we patiently endure no matter the length and no matter the severity of the trial. We surrender ourselves to God during the time of testing giving God complete control of the results. We keep on praying. We keep on trusting. We stand on the promises of God.

Throughout this book you will see me stress the importance of knowing God's Word. This goes beyond a casual reading every now and then. This requires intentionality. Why? Because time and time again in His Word we are told that life is not going to always be easy. James tells us to Count it all joy WHEN we face trials of many kinds… **John 16:33** tells us that in this life you WILL have tribulation…**Romans 12:12** admonishes us to be patient IN tribulation…**I Peter 4:12** says, Beloved, do not be surprised at the fiery trial WHEN it comes upon you to test you, as though something strange were happening to you. **Psalm 34:19** says, MANY are the afflictions of the righteous... Get the picture. Trials are inevitable but not insurmountable.

Valley living becomes doable because we have God on our side. **James 1: 3-4** says, for you know that the testing of your faith produces steadfastness. And let steadfastness have its full effect, that you may be perfect and complete, lacking in nothing. The B part of **John 16:33** says, but be of good cheer, I have overcome the world. **I Peter 4:13** says, *But rejoice insofar as you share Christ's sufferings, that you may also rejoice and be glad when his glory is revealed.* **Psalm 34:19b** says, but the Lord delivers him out of them all.

One thing we can always rest on is that God has a proven track record. The Bible is full of testimonies of the faithfulness of God. He never leaves His children alone. It may look like you are in an impossible situation, a Red Sea in front of you and Pharaoh's army behind you, God is still right there. You may be the choice for lunch on the lion's menu in a foreign country, but God is there. You may be considered kindle to keep the fire burning, just know that God has never left your side. You may be charged with leading a group of people into unknown territory and conquering occupied space, but God has said to you, *"Have I not commanded you? Be strong and courageous. Do not be frightened, and do not be dismayed, for the LORD your God is with you wherever you go."* **Joshua 1:9**

Here is what I want you to remember. There is nothing wrong with living in the valley. It is the experiences in the valley that helps make us into who God created us to be all along, Life was not meant to be lived on the mountaintop. For every mountaintop experience, we must climb back down to our regular place of dwelling. Success is achieved when we make peace with our regular place of residence in the valley and we realize that even in the valley we can enjoy the abundant life Jesus promised us. **John 10:10**

Principle #3

Don't be so quick to leave the valley, mountain climbing is not for the weak and requires an extensive training regime.

For everyone who sets off to climb a mountain, preparation must take place. You don't just get up one morning, put on some jeans and tennis shoes, drive to the foot of a mountain and then take off climbing. There are things one must do to be prepared.

One thing that must be done is you must read the Climbing Code. A climbing code is not meant to be a step-by-step formula for reaching summits or avoiding danger, but, rather; a set of guidelines for encouraging safe mountaineering. The Climbing Code for every Christian is the Bible. We enter this world sinners in need of a Savior. At some point in our lives we are introduced to who Jesus is and we make the decision to accept Him as our personal Lord and Savior. And then what? Does this mean everything in our life is now good? Does that mean every bad habit we have is now gone? Does that mean we will no longer lie, cheat, or steal? Does that mean we will now love everyone and become a mini-God on the earth?

No, it does not. What it means is that now we have a different set of guidelines to live by. We once lived by the world's guidelines and now we have changed sides and must live by what God says. **II Timothy 3:16-17** tells us that *"All Scripture is breathed out by God and profitable for teaching, for reproof, for correction, and for training in righteousness, that the man of God may be complete, equipped for every good work."* If you are to know what God requires of us, then we must read the Bible. If you want to learn how to live in the will of God and walk in the ways of God, you must read the Word of God.

The Bible is where we learn about God's heart for us. It is in the Bible that we find verses like **John 3:16,** *"For God so loved the world, that he gave his only Son, that whoever believes in him should not perish but have eternal life."* **and Romans 5:8** that tells us *"but God shows his love for us in that while we were still sinners, Christ died for us.*

It is in the Bible where we find the Ten Commandments. **(Exodus 20)**

It is in that same Bible where we find we are no longer under the law but under grace. **(Romans 6:14)**

It is in the Bible where we find what God wants for His children. **(Jeremiah 29:11; Psalm 23)**

It is in the Bible where we find instructions for daily living. **(Luke 10:27; Ephesians 4:17-32)**

It is in the Bible where we find how to get to the mountaintop. **(Matthew 17:1-9; Luke 9:27-36)**

Do you see how all this is working together? There is a process that God set up. A process that

Justification

To

Sanctification

To

Glorification

begins with justification and then moves to sanctification and finally to glorification. Sanctification is where all who are reading this book find ourselves today. It is the Word of God that walks us through the sanctification process when we find ourselves going through the process of teaching, reproof, correction, and training in righteousness. Let's look at each of these areas.

What is the Bible designed to teach us? While there are many things the Bible is designed to teach us, I will only address three. The Bible is designed to teach about God's love for us. The Bible teaches us about suffering. And finally, the Bible gives us a message of hope.

God's Love

From Genesis to Revelation we see God's love for mankind. God created Adam and Eve and placed them in the Garden of Eden. In the Garden everything they needed was provided. And even after they disobeyed God and sin entered the world a plan began for God to redeem us and bring us back to Him. Why did He do this? The answer is simple. He did it because He loves us.

Take a journey of love with me through the Old Testament. The children of Israel repeatedly rejected and disobeyed God and yet God continued to love them. In Exodus 32 we find the story of the golden calf, the idol they created after being delivered out of Egypt. And yet in **Exodus 34:6-7a** we find these words spoken by God Himself. *"The Lord, the Lord, a God merciful and gracious, slow to anger, and abounding in steadfast love and faithfulness, 7 keeping steadfast love for thousands, forgiving iniquity and transgression and sin..."*

In Jeremiah 32 we find a conversation between Jeremiah and the Lord while he was being held captive in Judah by King Zedekiah. In this chapter we find Jeremiah praying for understanding. He has seen firsthand the unfaithfulness of the children of Israel and yet is troubled by the instructions God has given him. God's reply is simple. Yes, captivity will come upon my people allowed by me. And even after all this He says in verses 40-41, *I will make with them an everlasting covenant, that I will not turn away from doing good to them. And I will put the fear of me in their hearts, that they may not turn from me. [41] I will rejoice in doing them good, and I will plant them in this land in faithfulness, with all my heart and all my soul.*

And in one of my all-time favorite stories in the Bible, the story of Hosea and Gomer, God uses their relationship to illustrate the way God will never turn His back on His people and will continue to love them no matter what. Gomer was a promiscuous woman, a whore, a harlot. Yet we find the Lord telling Hosea to choose her as his bride. And so, by divine appointment we find the daughter of Diblaim, became the unlikely wife of an up and coming young preacher. Now you would think that Hosea's love for her would cause her to turn away from her former life, but it didn't. It was not long before Gomer returned to her life of promiscuity, rejecting the love of her dear husband. And while Hosea had every right to divorce her, it is in

Hosea 3:1 we find these words. *"And the Lord said to me, "Go again, love a woman who is loved by another man and is an adulteress, even as the Lord loves the children of Israel, though they turn to other gods and love cakes of raisins."* And Hosea did just that. The same way God continued to forgive and love the children of Israel after they disappointed Him time and time again.

Then let's move to the New Testament. It is in the New Testament that we find the ultimate testament of God's love for us in that He sent His only begotten Son to earth as a perfect sacrifice to die on the cross for your sins and mine. There are some that try to belittle the sacrifice God made because while He was here on the earth He was still God. The part they fail to point out is He was also all man. It is in the Bible that we find the words written in **Hebrews 4:15,** *"For we do not have a high priest who is unable to* *sympathize with our weaknesses, but one who in every respect has been tempted as we are, yet without sin."* And I will even take it a step further to say that after experiencing the people on this earth firsthand I don't know that I would have completed my assignment. While on this earth **Isaiah 53:3** rang true. *"He was despised and rejected by men, a man of sorrows and acquainted with grief;"*

Yet one dark Friday they led Him up Golgotha's hill. They put nails in His hands and nails in His feet. They pierced Him in the side and put a crown of thorns upon His head. He stayed on that cross and from the sixth to the ninth hour darkness fell upon the face of the earth. That moment God had to close His eyes to the suffering of His only Son. And as the song says, 'He could have called ten thousand angels' to come and save Him. Yet, He decided to die. It wasn't the nails that kept my Savior up on that old rugged cross. It was His love. And there were sixty-six books written to share about that love.

Suffering

The second theme the Bible was designed to teach us is about suffering. Not one of us is exempt from suffering. I don't care how good you live. I don't care how much you pray or how often you read the Bible, we all must suffer. **II Timothy 3:12 says,** *"Indeed, all who desire to live a godly life will be persecuted..."* **Philippians 1:29 says,** *"For it has been granted to you that for the sake of Christ you should not only believe in him but also suffer for his sake..."* It was Paul who went on to say in **Philippians 3:10, "that I may know him and the power of his resurrection, and may share his sufferings, becoming like him in death..."**

Contrary to what many who profess a hope in Jesus Christ and proclaim the Good News of the gospel of Jesus Christ are teaching and preaching about right now, God did not send His Son so that we would have a happy, comfortable life. Au contraire mon frère. God's desire for His children is that we live a holy life. The path by which we get to living a holy life is not a clear path. It is one paved with difficulties, obstacles, hardships, and persecution. And the reason why we must endure these things is because of the first theme we discussed. God loves us. He loves us too much to leave us the way we are.

God did not send His Son so that we would have a happy, comfortable life.

I love jewelry. I am not rich, so I don't own many pieces of real, expensive jewelry. However, every now and then I go by the jewelry store and admire the diamond rings. (Secretly hoping one day someone might buy me one.) I love to look at the rings under the special lighting the jewelry stores have. This lighting is designed to showcase the brightness of the diamond causing you to want to make a purchase. In talking with a jeweler one day I discovered that no amount of lighting will hide a fake diamond and there are other tests the diamond must undergo to prove its authenticity. And this is after the excruciating process it must undergo to bring out it's true value before it is even placed in a gold ring setting.

A diamond starts out as a piece of coal. For it to become a diamond it must endure high pressure and high temperature. Before this happens there is a process called diamond mining involving a lot of digging and collecting. The next step in the process is crushing. During the crushing process large chunks of kimberlite are broken up into more easily transportable segments. After the crushing process comes separation. During separation the actual diamonds must be separated from the rock that surrounds them. Greasing then allows any remaining non-diamond particles to be rinsed away. And finally, we have cutting where a cleaving iron is used and with a quick, forceful blow, the diamond should split perfectly along its naturally occurring planes.

Nothing about that process sounds exciting or fun. In fact, all of it sounds painful. But then the jeweler began to show me the results of that painful process and I realize it was worth it all. At times it is hard for us to couple suffering with God's love. However, I want you to consider this. Do you think that God did not love His Son when He sent Him to die on the cross for us? None of us have been asked to physically die for our belief in Jesus. We have been asked to die to the flesh and become alive in Christ. We have been asked to **"put to death therefore what is earthly in you: sexual immorality, impurity, passion, evil desire, and covetousness, which is idolatry."** We have been told to **"put away anger, wrath, malice, slander, and obscene talk from your mouth."** **(Colossians 3:5;8)** And I hate to break it to you, but this doesn't come naturally. Only God knows what we must go through for us to be the sons and daughters He created us to be. We must suffer in order that we may be made better.

Therefore, don't run away from suffering. **II Timothy 2:3 says, *"Share in suffering as a good soldier of Christ Jesus."*** When you became a Christian, you were then enlisted in the army of the Lord. God became your Commander-in-Chief and all your orders come directly from Him. There will be times you will be led into enemy camps. There will be times you will undergo injury because of friendly fire. Sickness may come. Injury may come. One thing is sure that there will never be a time when you are not in active duty because the Bible tells us that the devil, enemy number one, *"prowls around like a roaring lion, seeking someone to devour."* **(I Peter 5:8b)** This is why we must *"Put on the whole armor of God, that you may be able to stand against the schemes of the devil."* **(Ephesians 6:11)**

Hope

One thing I love about the Bible is the message of hope written on the pages within. Whenever I read the Bible I am reminded God's love never fails. I am also reminded there is a purpose behind the pain. Both statements give me hope. If God had said endure suffering just because and yet remain the same, I would question this thing called Christianity. If God would have said, "I love you only as long as you do things my way" and not offered us grace and mercy I would not be so gung ho about sharing the Good News of Jesus Christ. Verse after verse tells us that when we do things God's way we will receive a reward. Sometimes the reward will be immediate. Ultimately the reward will be received in heaven.

There are two passages of Scripture in the Bible that are staples in my life: **II Corinthians 4:16-18** (one of my life verses) and **Romans 8:31-39**. I suggest reading them and adding them to your spiritual treasure chest. For this study I want to look at **Romans 8:31-39**.

What then shall we say to these things? If God is for us, who can be against us? [32] He who did not spare his own Son but gave him up for us all, how will he not also with him graciously give us all things? [33] Who shall bring any charge against God's elect? It is God who justifies. [34] Who is to condemn? Christ Jesus is the one who died—more than that, who was raised—who is at the right hand of God, who indeed is interceding for us. [35] Who shall separate us from the love of Christ? Shall tribulation, or distress, or persecution, or famine, or nakedness, or danger, or sword? [36] As it is written,

"For your sake we are being killed all the day long; we are regarded as sheep to be slaughtered."

[37] No, in all these things we are more than conquerors through him who loved us. [38] For I am sure that neither death nor life, nor angels nor rulers, nor things present nor things to come, nor powers, [39] nor height nor depth, nor anything else in all creation, will be able to separate us from the love of God in Christ Jesus our Lord.

If you ever wrap your mind around the thought that everything God allows to happen in your life is because God loves you, your life will be much more peaceful. When you understand that it doesn't matter who is against you because God is for you. That absolutely no one can bring any charges against you because Christ Jesus Himself does not. That there is absolutely nothing that can separate you from the love of God.

I remember when I became pregnant with my son, Khalil. I was embarrassed and ashamed. I wasn't concerned really with what anyone thought except my daddy. I dreaded telling him. In fact, I remember calling him even though I could have easily gone to his house and told him. I just didn't want to see the look of disappointment on his face. I didn't want him to think less of me. I didn't want him to stop loving me. Funny thing is when I called him, his response was as though he already knew. He let me get the words out and then he asked me when my first doctor's appointment was. I told him, and he said okay remind me, so I can go. The next thing he said was "I bet you're hungry. Let's go eat tomorrow." He didn't beat me down about my mistake. He realized that was the last thing I needed. What I needed most, he gave. A father's unconditional love. This is precisely what God does for us. God is not happy with us when we sin. Yes, at times, He must punish us for the wrong we commit. However, even in punishment, He never stops loving us. A fact that gives us hope.

Before I leave this topic of hope and what the Bible teaches us I want to leave you with some verses to encourage you. These are verses that over the years I have memorized and during some of my darkest days I was reminded that God has not forgotten me.

But they who wait for the Lord shall renew their strength; they shall mount up with wings like eagles; they shall run and not be weary; they shall walk and not faint. **Isaiah 40:31**

And after you have suffered a little while, the God of all grace, who has called you to his eternal glory in Christ, will himself restore, confirm, strengthen, and establish you. **I Peter 5:10**

We are afflicted in every way, but not crushed; perplexed, but not driven to despair; [9] persecuted, but not forsaken; struck down, but not destroyed; [10] always carrying in the body the death of Jesus, so that the life of Jesus may also be manifested in our bodies. **II Corinthians 4:8-10**

When you pass through the waters, I will be with you; and through the rivers, they shall not overwhelm you; when you walk through fire you shall not be burned, and the flame shall not consume you. **Isaiah 43:2**

It is good for me that I was afflicted, that I might learn your statutes. **(Psalm 119:71)**

Blessed is the man who remains steadfast under trial, for when he has stood the test he will receive the crown of life, which God has promised to those who love him. **James 1:12**

These are just a few of the verses I treasure. I encourage you to pull out your Bible and develop your own list of verses you can stand on in times of doubt, discouragement, and even depression.

The next word we want to dissect from II Timothy 3:16 is **reproof**. Another word you can place here is conviction. Through the power of the Holy Spirit the Word of God should convict us. Conviction first takes place when we discover that we cannot save ourselves. And that is no small task. There are many people in the world today who believe they do not need God. They believe that they can do everything for themselves. They believe everything they have is because of what they have done. They don't believe in heaven or hell.

Once we are saved it is through the Word of God we discover attitudes and behaviors that are not of God that must be corrected. A lot of us have the head knowledge of sin; however, we don't surrender to the Holy Spirit when He tries to convict us of our individual sin to bring about changed behavior.

On a more positive note the Word of God serves to convict us or better yet convince us of the truth. Verses like *"There is therefore now no condemnation for those who are in Christ Jesus."* **Romans 8:1** and *"I give them eternal life, and they will never perish, and no one will snatch them out of my hand."* **John 10:28** One of the primary ways the devil attacks us is in our minds. That is why we are commanded to *"Set* *your minds on things that are above, not on things that are on earth."* **Colossians 3:2**

The enemy will have you believing you are unworthy, and that God doesn't love you. The enemy will continue to place people in your path that try and hold that one thing against you, that although true, God has forgiven you. He will have you believing God shows favoritism. The enemy will have you believing everyone is against you. Have I come down your street yet? We need to give the Bible it's proper value. When we read the Word of God, we need to read it as though God is speaking, because He is! Those are not just words on a page. These are words God felt we needed to help us walk through life. Stop letting the devil convince you otherwise.

In 2001 I was in the hospital for seven days for trying to harm myself. I didn't want to live anymore. The devil had convinced me I was all alone, and no one loved me. All the verses I had memorized as a child had gone right out the window. **Matthew 28:20b**, *"And behold, I am with you always, to the end of the age."* Gone. **Hebrews 13:5b**, *"for he has said, "I will never leave you nor forsake you."* Gone. **Deuteronomy 31:6**, *"Be strong and courageous. Do not fear or be in dread of them, for it is the LORD your God who goes with you. He will not leave you or forsake you."* Gone. The only thing rolling around in my mind were thoughts of negativity. I was involved in my own pity party. I shut myself off from everyone. I wasn't going to church. I wasn't praying. I wasn't reading my Bible. I had the negative record on repeat.

While in the hospital I wasn't allowed to have anything. Everything was considered an instrument I could use to do harm to myself.

During the day everyone had to come out into a common area and sit. The first couple of days I just sat there. On the third day I asked the nurse if I could have a Bible. She said yes. That day I sat there and begin to read. I don't remember exactly what I read. I do remember, however, beginning to feel peace. As I sat there and listened to God speak to me I was convinced once again of God's love for me. I was reminded this was just a small part of my journey and God still had great things in store for me. I was reminded of the promise he made me at a very early age. I left that hospital convinced my life was worth living.

This episode did not cure me of my lifelong battle with depression and anxiety. It simply reminded me that God's grace is sufficient. That God will sustain me through whatever battle I must face.

The third word we will look at is **correction**. Here the word means leading to an amendment of life, a reformation. Of all the tools designed to get people on the straight and narrow, the Bible is still the most effect instrument. Any change that is not based on the Word of God soon becomes ill-effective.

The Bible is the most effective tool for correction.

What does the Word of God say about correction?

Hebrews 12:11 says, *"For the moment all discipline seems painful rather than pleasant, but later it yields the peaceful fruit of righteousness to those who have been trained by it."*

Proverbs 3:11-12 says, *"My son, do not despise the LORD's discipline or be weary of his* *reproof, for the LORD reproves him whom he loves, as a father the son in whom he delights."*

Correction is necessary. I know nothing about boating. I do, however, watch all these weird shows on television at night when I can't sleep. One night I found myself intrigued by a show on boating. What intrigued me the most was how important it is to stay on course. Even the slightest change from the course will leave you lost at sea. And there is nothing worse than being stuck in the middle of the ocean. The same is true when it comes to our Christian walk. There is danger when our lives veer from the path God set for us. Getting too far off course can lead to disaster and even destruction.

Before we move forward in this discussion, let me correct something. God does not correct us through sickness and pain. He does not punish us with emotional, physical or financial distress.

For everyone who was told the reason they were going through what they were going through was God was punishing them, I am sorry. That is not true. God loves us perfectly and more completely than anyone on this earth ever could. His love and our salvation does not isolate us from trials and tribulations. His love and our salvation does shield us from destruction.

So, if God's correction is not punishment then what is it? Picture this. A loving father bending down and having a conversation with his son about the things he continues to do that breaks his heart. Not only does he share how and why it breaks his heart. He continues by telling him the harm it is doing to his own life. He then gives him suggestions on how to stop the behavior and even things to replace the bad behavior with. Correction is used to help us grow and mature in our faith. When the Bible refers to correction from God, this is what it means. God speaks to us through His Holy Word with gentleness. Say this with me. "God wants what is best for me. Correction is one of the ways he gives me what is best for me."

God understands we receive enough scrutiny from those in the world. We have those that want to see us fail and will even set traps for us hoping we fail. There are times when God allows us to fail, not calling us failures; but allowing us to fail in order that we might draw nearer to Him. He understands we are dust. He knows we are not perfect but being perfected. This does not give us a license to continue in the bad behavior. In fact, it is the Father's love for us that should cause us to run into His arms eager to hear whatever He says. There will be times when we will veer off course and like the captain of a ship, God works to guide us back on course.

The final way the Word of God is profitable for is **training in righteousness**. Before we look at these words together let's begin by looking at them separately.

To train is about more than teaching. To train involves proper development of the skills necessary to perform a task. Training prepares you.

Righteousness is a characteristic of God. Often, it refers to ethical conduct. Sinners are declared righteous by the Father through the Son. This is where we get the term imputed righteousness. Christians are then made righteous through the work of the Holy Spirit and eventually we will be fully righteous in the time to come. It is **Philippians 1:6** which says, *"And I am sure of this, that he who began a good work in you will bring it to completion at the day of Jesus Christ."*

So, my question is if righteousness comes from God alone what is meant by the term training in righteousness. It means that everything we need for Godly living we can find it in the Word of God. The Bible teaches us how to resist temptation, pray, and worship. The Bible commands us to tell others about Jesus and then tells us how to do it. Training is the practical application that takes place. It is that transition we make in obedience to **James 1:22** which tells us, *"But be doers of the word, and not hearers only, deceiving yourselves."*

There is a prayer I pray every Sunday and Wednesday night. I pray God speaks to me personally and whatever He says He will help me to put it into practice. I haven't always prayed this prayer. It began after a conversation with my oldest daughter. Every Sunday after church we have a conversation about the sermon and they must tell me at least one practical point. They cannot just repeat back to me the points they copied down from the screen. They must tell me how that point applies to them where they are now. One particular Sunday I began the conversation and my daughter said, "Mom I don't have anything today. He has been talking about the same thing for over a month. I got it by now. We need to be sure of our salvation."

When I got home I thought about what she said. It is very easy for a Christian to become familiar with the Bible. Before the preacher even reads the text, we know what it says, and we think we already know what his points will be and the life application. I realized that I, too, have been guilty of this. Sometimes I will try to fill in the blanks without even hearing the sermon. This practice was however causing me to miss out on what God was trying to say to me in this season of my life. Have you ever read a Scripture in the

Bible, maybe one that you learned when you were young, and this time it means something totally different?

Training in righteousness never ends. The Bible was not designed to be read cover to cover one time and then we have everything that we need. Just as a human being goes through different developmental stages, so do we as Christians. We begin as babes in Christ and grow into mature Christians, no longer drinking milk out of the bottle but able to chew and digest meat. We should never approach the reading of Scripture as though we already know what it says. In fact, I will take it one step further and say we should never read the Bible without praying first. As we train, we become stronger, wiser, better.

Here is one other point I want to make. While training what you avoid is just as important as what you take in. A few years ago, my best friend and I signed up to run our very first 5K, The Hot Mama Run. Yes, you read that correctly. Neither one of us had every ran a 5K so training was essential. The very first thing I did was go online to find training routines already out there that I could add to my regular workout routine. Then I added an app on my phone that I could use when I spent time at the track. The very first training plan I read mentioned your diet. While training I would need to cut out sweets and my favorite, Diet Dr. Pepper. I needed to have a healthy diet of fruits and vegetable and fried foods in moderation. I did not want to hear this. The reason why I worked out was so I could eat whatever I wanted. I knew what my daily calorie intake should be and if I went over I knew that meant I just had to burn more calories that day when I went to the gym. I had it all worked out. I didn't like this plan, so I clicked on the next one. As I clicked on four or five different training plans they all said the same thing. There were certain foods and drinks I could not have during this period of training.

The same thing is true for every Christian. Yes, we may pray and read our Bible. We may attend church on Sunday and Bible Study during the week. The question remains what are you taking in the rest of your day? What are you watching on television? Who do you follow on social media? Who do you spend most of your time talking to? While you may believe you are strong enough to differentiate between the good and the bad, the truth and a lie, positivity and negativity, I would venture to say those things influence your life. I tell my children all the time 'garbage in, garbage out'. They hate when I regulate what they can watch on television. They don't like that I control who they follow on social media. The funniest thing was when my youngest daughter set up her Instagram account and I went out there and saw she had over five hundred friends. She didn't even know five hundred people, so I made her delete them and start all over.

As you read the Word of God and it truly becomes a part of you, there will be things you can no longer stomach. It doesn't make you better than anyone. It just means you are on a path that says you want to live a life that pleases God. It means you read the Word as a mirror designed to expose anything that is not like God. You have moved past comparing yourself to other imperfect people and have set your eyes on the finish line to become more and more like Christ each day.

Growing up I remember watching a commercial that said "when E.F. Hutton speaks, people listen." I remember one commercial where two gentlemen were sitting in a restaurant having dinner discussing the purchase of a stock. At one point in the commercial one of the men says his stock broker agreed that it would be a good investment. The other man proceeded to ask who his stockbroker was to which the man replied "E.F. Hutton." Suddenly, the restaurant went silent. The band stopped playing and everyone shifted their position to better hear what the man was going to say next.

The Bible is GOD SPEAKING.

This is how we as Christians should be when we read the Word of God. God is speaking, and every word is of value to us. Whether or not we like what it says or agree with what it says, it is profitable. We can't just read the Old Testament avoiding the New Testament. We must read the Bible as one book designed to perfect and equip us for every good work. Through Scripture we learn what is true, what is wrong, how to correct the wrong, and how to apply the truth.

"All Scripture is breathed out by God and profitable for teaching, for reproof, for correction, and for training in righteousness, that the man of God may be complete, equipped for every good work." (II Timothy 3:16-17)

Principle # 4:

You can experience the mountaintop while living in the valley.

Mountaintop experiences are not about location; they are about perspective. It is about position. One of the most quoted passages in the Bible is **Romans 8:28**.

"And we know that all things work together for the good of them who love God, who are the called according to His purpose."

Notice I said one of the most quoted Scriptures, not one of the most believed. We love to shout about this verse a year after the layoff, five years after the divorce when we are walking down the aisle, ten years after we buried our loved one. After all, hindsight is 20/20. I can see the good now that I am on a better job. I can see the good now that my Adam or my Eve has arrived. I can see the good now that I can smile at the good times I shared with mama or daddy. What are we saying when twelve months later I'm still unemployed with no savings? Car has been repossessed and I just received an eviction notice. What are you saying when your ex is the one walking down the aisle with someone else and you are barely making ends meet? What are you saying when you are still overwhelmed by grief so much so that you have shrunk into a state of depression? For most people **Romans 8:28** only applies when the God's plan matches up with their plan. Our inability to quote and believe this verse is a lack of faith.

Years ago, when I began studying the Word of God I was given some advice by one of the best Bible teachers I know. His words to me were as follows. "There are no standalone verses. Learn how to study each verse in context. Read what comes before the verse then read what comes after the verse."

Let us begin by looking at the preceding verses.

Likewise, the Spirit helps us in our weakness. For we do not know what to pray for as we ought, but the Spirit himself intercedes for us with groanings too deep for words. [27] And he who searches hearts knows what is the mind of the Spirit, because the Spirit intercedes for the saints according to the will of God. [28] And we know that for those who love God all things work together for good, for those who are called according to his purpose.

The Apostle Paul begins by informing us of our condition. All of us will experience moments of weakness. There will be times when we don't know what to do. There will be times when our faith will fail us. There will be times when what we see with our physical eyes will confuse us. As children of God we have been taught that this is when we are to pray. But here Paul tells us that during these times we don't know what to pray for. When we are weak, we are not competent enough to judge our condition accurately.

When my father was diagnosed with cancer my siblings' prayer was only that my father be healed. You may be reading this saying well what is wrong with that? On the surface there is nothing wrong with that. It is in Exodus 15 we learn that God is Jehovah Rapha, the God who heals. The problem is they did not include in their prayers "not my will but Thy will be done". It was a selfish prayer not taking my father's pain into consideration nor the greater purpose for my father's pain. There was no thought as to how God would be glorified.

Ecclesiastes 6:12a says, *"For who knows what is good for man while he lives the few days of* *his vain lie, which he passes like a shadow?"* By nature, we favor our flesh. Because of this our prayers are going to include requests that lessen the amount of pain and pressure. Who prays "Lord please inflict whatever pain necessary on my life so that I will become more like you?" No one. However, that is exactly what our prayer should be.

Another reason this is not our request is because we tend to think more highly of ourselves than we ought to think. At times, we believe we are further along than we really are. I remember the very first time I had a facial at the spa. Prior to going I had always been told how beautiful my skin was. It wasn't until this day did I realize looks could be deceiving.

I grew up in the days of Ivory soap. Every morning I would wake up and wash my face. I carried this practice with me into adulthood. I refused to use any type of skin care products or facials in a bottle because my mother said all those products would damage my skin not help it.

Before my facial I told the esthetician my fear. I then went on to tell her I didn't feel I needed a facial. After listening to me she asked if she could show me something. She pulled out a white pad, poured a liquid substance on it and then rubbed it on my face.

Think for a minute about the most trying time in your life; the time when the situation made you feel that God seemed absent. If you prayed, what was your prayer? Maybe you heard rumors of layoffs and you begin to pray you would not be on that list. Perhaps your wife served you with divorce papers and you prayed God would give her a change of heart. Maybe you came home from work and there was an eviction notice on the door and you prayed God would give you the money to pay the rent, so you and your children would not have to move for the third time. Perhaps the follow-up visit to the doctor said the cancer had returned and you pray Lord let this be an error.

You prayed and went to sleep and when you woke up the next morning nothing had changed. You went to work and received your severance package. Your wife was gone when you returned home. There was no unexpected check in the mail. The nurse called to schedule the chemotherapy treatments once again. You cry out "Why now God?" All this is happening when I am serving you. I have been doing pretty good. There are a few things I still struggle with but for the most part I am on the battlefield for my Lord. So again, you ask, "Why now God?"

Just as the cleaning agent the esthetician used was able to reveal dirt that was invisible to the physical eye. God's omniscience can see things in us that are not like Him that need to be removed. God is also able to see those things we lack and knows precisely how to build those things up in us.

Paul tells us in *Galatians 5:19-21 that the works of the flesh are sexual immorality, impurity, sensuality, [20] idolatry, sorcery, enmity, strife, jealousy, fits of anger, rivalries, dissensions, divisions, [21] envy, drunkenness, orgies, and things like these."* We don't grow into these things. We are born with them. They are a part of your very nature. This is not an all-inclusive list but a comprehensive list. It covers four important categories: sensual sins, superstitious sins, temperament sins, and sins of excess. Paul is not saying you will commit all these sins. He is just saying because we are born in sin and shapen in iniquity, you are just a step away. And if we catch you on a bad day we may catch you falling right into the sin.

Love
Joy
Peace
Patience
Kindness
Goodness
Faithfulness
Gentleness
Self-Control

God wants us to avoid these things. He wants us to object to these things. And we can, but only with God. Many of us suffer from a heart condition and God must perform open heart surgery. He wants to take out our bad heart and replace it with a heart like His. One that lives by the Spirit and walks in the Spirit. He longs to replace hate with love, unhappiness with joy, discord with peace, impatience with patience, that intolerance with kindness, cruelty with goodness, disloyalty with faithfulness, harshness with gentleness, and instability with self-control. Love, joy and peace are birthed out of relationship with God. Patience, kindness and goodness refers to our relationship with others. With love, joy and peace reigning in our lives we can walk in the next three elements of the fruit of the Spirit. Faithfulness, gentleness, and self-control refers to how we are to live in this fallen world. Through difficulties and opposition, we are always to represent God. We are to faithfully do the right thing. We don't always have to respond to opposition. We must exercise self-control when natural passions rise up in us.

None of these things come naturally. Not on the level God intended, a life led by the Spirit. We may love but it's not unconditional. We may know joy, but it is dependent upon our circumstances. We may have peace until something takes us off our routine. We are patient with a time-clock attached. We are kind when it serves our purpose. We extend goodness to those who are good to us or at least make us look good while being good. We are faithful to that which never disappoints us. We are hardly ever meek because it makes us look weak. And when it comes to self-control, it's go ahead and do it and ask for forgiveness later.

It is only when we are tried by the fire will we come forth as pure gold. I have never heard of a cold fire. Fire is always hot. The temperature of the fire can be controlled, but it is always hot. If you don't believe me light a match and stick your finger in it. I bet before too long you will be screaming "hot, hot, hot". What you can be grateful about is the one who controls the temperature is an all-wise and loving God.

Let me give you a piece of wisdom that has helped me tremendously through the years. Stop trying to figure out what God is doing. The best thing for you to do is put the car in neutral and enjoy the ride. As you ride along you may encounter a storm. Don't be a backseat driver. Don't try to take over the steering wheel. Don't pull over in the storm. Don't turn around and go back to where you started. Just keep going. The driver knows exactly how to get you to your destination. He will get you where you need to be at the right time. Don't be so quick to leave the valley and arrive at the mountain. One of the worse things you can do is arrive and not be prepared.

There was a time in my life when I felt like God had me on the fast track. Everything was going well. I had a few minor setbacks but for the most part everything was well. Then one day BAM! The tsunami hit. What I thought I had on the inside proved false. As I look back on that period of my life I know now I was not yet ready for what God had promised me. The life He had shown me I would have fumbled the ball.

Confirmation of this very thing came almost fifteen years later when I was asked to speak at a Women's Conference. After speaking one of the mentors of the Young Adult District Women, who I was privileged to lead, came up to me and said. "I am so proud of you. I wanted to tell you then you were not ready, but it would not have been received. Today I see God in you. I see life's experiences have shown you who God is." I hugged her and thanked her for those kind words.

People of God we are unable to judge our condition. Only God can. The best thing you can do is surrender to the process. Allow God to lead, guide and direct you through the twists and turns of life. Who would you rather have praying for you? Jesus says, "I and my Father are one."

This means Jesus can see down the road. Accept His love. Appreciate His heart for you. Acknowledge He knows best. Without this assistance you will not be able to endure.

The human language is unable to truly express what we feel. Think about this. You understand more about a person's grief through his or her sobs. Love is better expressed through the look in someone's eye or hand holding than with the three little words everyone always says they are dying to hear. If we are inadequate in expressing what we feel than would not the smart thing be to rely on the Spirit that dwells within us. We understand what we want the result to be, but we don't know what path to take to get there.

Every Christian should have a prayer of "Lord make me better." What we don't know is how? We may pray for something to happen one way and God answers it another way. Did you know that our seemingly unanswered prayers may just be the answers to our real prayers? Those prayers prayed by the Spirit who can discern our deepest longings.

I am often reminded of the story of Mary, Martha and Lazarus. I can only imagine when Lazarus died his sisters felt God had not answered their prayer. After all, they had sent word to Jesus. By the time Jesus arrived Lazarus had been dead four days. This is the same Jesus who had previously showed His love for them by dining at their table. Jesus, however, knew the answer to the real prayer. The real prayer was for Mary and Martha to come to know Jesus and the power of His resurrection. Not only was Jesus able to confirm the words He spoke in John 11 to Martha and Mary, there were others who would come to know of His power.

It is the Holy Spirit that supports us in our infirmities. One thing we can rest assured of is in our weakness we can rely on the Holy Spirit and rejoice in His presence. The Father listens because there is no doubt those groanings are in the will of God. The matter of what the will of God is for our lives is at times difficult for us. Praying according to the will of God, respects;

1. The subject of our prayers. (Matthew 6:10)

2. The style in which we pray. (Luke 11:2-4)

3. The solution we are praying for. (Jam 4:3)

Praying the will of God requires surrender.

I John 5:14-15 *And this is the confidence that we have toward him, that if we ask anything* *according to his will he hears us. [15] And if we know that he hears us in whatever we ask, we know that we have the requests that we have asked of him.*

The anything verse 14 refers to is not about God giving us things to make us happy, those temporal things that will fade away. The anything the Bible tells us repeatedly we can receive refers to moving God to His rightful place of being Lord of our lives. It means He moves from taking up temporary residence, renting a convenient space we make for him, to assuming permanent ownership. The things we want for ourselves no longer matters. What matters most is what God wants for our lives. From where I'm sitting right now this sounds simple but when it comes to putting this into action it becomes hard. Why? Because most of us have not totally surrendered our lives to God. Yes, we are saved but God doesn't have total control of our lives. He has control on Sundays and Wednesdays. He has control when the cameras are on but not when the cameras are off. He has control just so long as His plan fits with what we want. Just think about it. We love to shout about Romans 8:28 and what we know, that all things work together for the good. The question is do we still consider it good when God's plan is not what we have planned for ourselves? Or do we consider it good when it is contrary to what we want because an all-wise, all-powerful God deemed it so. He is the one who knows us better than we know ourselves and the One qualified to make decisions.

If I were to take a poll, I would venture to say most of us have been living a life that says we think we know what is best for our lives. That is why we begin things and we don't consult God. What we do instead is ask Him to bless it after the fact.

Seventeen years ago, I married the father of my three beautiful girls. After much time in conversation with God I realized I didn't consult God before the union was made. I made the decision on my own. It made sense. We looked good together. We fit. He was the Assistant to the Pastor and I was the up and coming leader and speaker of the Young Adult women. Because of my decision I have four children who have had to suffer. My subsequent prayer was "God please fix my marriage." Yes, He could have but that would mean two individuals would have had to surrender themselves totally to the Lord and allow God to make them over so that we could be a better husband and wife to one another. And at that time neither one of us was ready to do that. One would think I learned my lesson from this mistake. But what did I do? I got married again without consulting God. This time I didn't even seek a Godly man. My attitude was if the first marriage didn't work and He was a man of the church, let me try someone far away from the church. That decision was not good either. It also ended in divorce.

Surrender is a battle term. It means giving up all rights to the Conqueror. In battle when someone surrenders they lay down their arms, anything and everything that can be used against the conquering party acknowledging I am now under your total control. It's the same with us when we give our lives over to Christ. That means we give up our plans and our wants and replace them with what God wants for us. And furthermore, we don't do it grudgingly we do it eagerly.

Romans 12:1 *I appeal to you therefore, brothers, by the mercies of God, to present your bodies as a living sacrifice, holy and acceptable to God, which is your spiritual worship.*

Galatians 2:20 *I have been crucified with Christ. It is no longer I who live, but Christ who lives in me. And the life I now live in the flesh I live by faith in the Son of God, who loved me and gave himself for me.*

Luke 22:42 *"Father, if you are willing, remove this cup from me. Nevertheless, not my will, but yours, be done."*

Salvation is about more than going to heaven or being saved from hell.

Your decision to accept Jesus Christ as your personal Lord and Savior was not just about going to heaven. Your decision enlisted you in the army of the Lord. It moved you from an enemy of God to His friend. It made God your Commander-in-Chief. Your orders come from Him. Sometimes He requires you to go some places you don't want to go and endure some hardships you think are unfair. You must keep in mind following His every instruction is the key to your winning not just when you get to Heaven but also the key to living an abundant life while you are still here on this earth.

After you surrender your will, the next step to praying God's will is knowing God's will. You must have proper scholarship. I have had many people ask me "How do I know what God's will is for my life?" My response is always do you read the Bible? One of the primary purposes of the Bible is to show us God's will for our lives. Did you know the purpose of prayer was never to serve our own needs but to further the kingdom of God? Yes, our needs are met through prayer, but it is, so we can then serve God better and more fully. When we are full of the Word it will flow into our prayers and we won't have to wonder if it is God's Will. We won't become frustrated when it seems God hasn't answered our prayers because we know what the Word of God says.

John 15:7 says *"If you abide in me, and my words abide in you, ask whatever you wish, and it will be done for you."*

Bottom line we need to be so full of the Word of God that it comes pouring from our lips to God's ears. We will know His likes and dislikes. We will know His character. We will know God's heart and when we pray it goes beyond bless me and Bless my family. Now I lay me down to sleep. Lord I need more money. Lord heal my body. It moves to a prayer that includes salvation for others, healing for others, forgiveness of our sins, asking God to remove from us the ugly that the Scripture has exposed during our time in the Word. It involves sacrificing that one thing we want most for that thing we didn't know we needed until God told us that we did. It involves a prayer of thanksgiving in all circumstances. In difficulties. In distress. In discouragement. In disease.

Remember in Luke 22 when Jesus told Peter the devil desires to sift you as wheat, but I have prayed for you. Jesus could have prayed that Peter not be sifted but instead he prayed Peter's faith not fail, that after he be restored and finally that he would strengthen his brothers. Our prayers should not always be about getting out of something.

It is when we have *purposed surrender* and *proper scholarship* then we will be rewarded with a *perfect solution*.

God is not in Heaven looking down on us trying to make our lives miserable. He loves us and only wants what's best for us. Prayer is the greatest privilege for every Christian. Prayer is also most often the greatest failure for every Christian. Why?

1. Because we have not because we ask not. (James 4:2)

2. Because we ask with wrong motives. (James 4:3)

Flip the record over and play the other side and we find answered prayers that we are satisfied with because we have full confidence in the One who made the decision.

If God answered yes, He had a good reason. Hallelujah! We're ecstatic!

If God answered no, He had a good reason. One of the main reasons God answers no is because of the sin in our lives. We must search our hearts, confess and repent. We often forget about the sin of unforgiveness. Forgetting that Jesus said, "but if you do not forgive others their trespasses, neither will your Father forgive your trespasses."

Matthew 6:15 Another reason God says no is He is protecting us. When will we figure out God can see things we cannot see. He knows all things. Why do you think the pilot is in constant contact with the tower not just while in the air but at takeoff and before landing? If it's not safe to take off the flight must be grounded. If it is not safe to land than the plane must circle in the air until they receive the all clear.

When they are in the air there are times when the plane must be directed over or around a storm to avoid turbulence. Sometimes the pilot has no choice but to fly through the storm telling the passengers to buckle up and brace themselves. The pilot doesn't make these decisions alone. He must rely on the tower. He keeps the radio on not just to ask questions but also to receive direction.

When you think about the times God has said no to you, I want you to think of it another way.

God's no isn't rejection it's redirection.

2 Corinthians 12:8-9 says: *Three times I pleaded with the Lord to take it away from me. But He said to me, "My grace is sufficient for you, for My power is made perfect in weakness."* Paul's response to this was: *"Therefore, I will boast all the more gladly about my weaknesses, so that Christ's power may rest on me. That is why, for Christ's sake, I delight in weaknesses, in insults, in hardships, in persecutions, in difficulties. For when I am weak, then I am strong."* **II Corinthians 12:9-10**

Paul did not arrive at this conclusion overnight. The Scripture says he begged the Lord three times and each time God said no. It does not tell

115

us if he pleaded with God three times in the same prayer or if was three different times. He doesn't tell us if the first time he asked God it was painful but not yet unbearable. The second time he was a little more passionate in his prayer because the pain was getting worse and he needed just a little relief. What we do know is the third time when he cried out to the Lord he just couldn't take it anymore. And even with his heart fully exposed and the intensity of his prayer did not move God to say yes. He did answer him though. He said to him, Paul, my grace is sufficient.

I have heard many people say God was telling Paul His grace was enough. However, the word enough doesn't do this justice. The word sufficient encompasses more than enough. It means 'adequate to the end proposed'. **Sufficiency is supply equal to our needs**. More than enough, grace is the proper remedy for all things. We may think the pain medication is enough. It will soon wear off. We may think the job is enough. We must remember it is the resource not the source. We may think our investments or our retirement is enough. What happens when the market crashes? Grace is God's unmerited favor and it will take care of all things to carry us through to the result God has purposed for each of us.

God's no isn't punishment it is preparation.

Romans 5:2-5 says, *"and we rejoice in hope of the glory of God. ³Not only that, but we rejoice in our sufferings, knowing that suffering produces endurance, ⁴ and endurance produces character, and character produces hope, ⁵ and hope does not put us to shame, because God's love has been poured into our hearts through the Holy Spirit who has been given to us."* Pain produces progress. Pain has purpose. I cannot stress enough that God's desire for His children is holiness.

If God said wait, He had a good reason. God's delays are not denials. My granny used to always say, "Stop opening that oven. Don't try to take the cake out of the oven too quickly. Give it enough time to cook all the way through." I'm sure there were moments when Joseph wondered why he was still sitting in that prison cell. Had not God shown him that he would be in a position of leadership and his family would bow down to him. I'm sure there were mornings when Abraham woke up next to Sarah and said are you pregnant yet? I'm sure Noah got tired of the people laughing at him while he was building the ark and yet no rain came. Oh but, when it finally happened in each of their lives, what a testament it was of the faithfulness of God. These stories were proof of Romans 8:28 before Paul ever wrote those words. Joseph went from the pit to

Potiphar's house to prison and then to the palace as second in command. In that position, Joseph was able to save his family from a famine. Abraham and Sarah gave birth to Isaac which was the beginning of the birth line that led to our Savior. One day Noah felt a drop of rain on his forehead and while he and his family were safe in the ark there were people on the outside perishing who had laughed at him and did not believe.

Whether it is yes, no or not yet it is still a perfect solution given by a perfect God. Although you won't always understand, prayer is still always essential for every Christian. We must persevere in prayer even when we don't understand God's will or His ways. *"For as the heavens are higher than the earth, so are my ways higher than your ways and my thoughts than your thoughts."* **Isaiah 55:9**

Prayer requires faith. Faith is confidence in the person of Jesus Christ and in his power, so that even when his power does not serve my end, my confidence in him remains because of who he is. And so, we keep on praying. Here is the thought I want to put on your mind today? Do you really believe in prayer or do you pray as a perfunctory act? Perfunctory means - "to perform a task with a minimum of effort, to do something with apathy; to be dispassionate, detached, halfhearted, indifferent, lukewarm, and spiritless. If we are honest with ourselves, we must own our struggle with the power of prayer. We must admit there are times when we say to ourselves, Is it worth it? Is it effective? How do I do it? Is there a right way or a wrong way? How do I know if I God really hears me? Why pray if God is just going to do what He wants anyway? Does any of that sound familiar?

Let's look at the other side of that. What happens if you don't pray? What happens if God really does hear and answer our prayers? Nothing supernatural happens without prayer. And many of us are wanting God to do something supernatural in our lives, something only a God who can do the impossible can make happen and yet we haven't prayed about it. And if we have prayed about it we haven't been persistent in our prayer or we prayed not really believing God would answer. The day I fully grasped what prayer is I was in one of the worst trials of my life. I didn't ask God to get me out of the trial. My prayer was simply, "God I don't know why this is happening, but You do. I trust You with the outcome. I know that when it is over I will be better, and I will have a testimony of Your goodness." In essence, I was praying, "God, I believe that this will work out for my good."

Principle #5

Do not fear the climb.

Dear children Satan is real. You probably read that opening sentence going, "Okay so why is she telling me this." Because most of us don't live our lives as though Satan is real. We treat the enemy as though he is a man dressed up in a red one-piece suit with horns, a tail, and a pitchfork. We journey through life as if we don't acknowledge the enemy that he does not exist. We would must rather blame people and things we can see for the problems in our life. We blame everything and everybody for the reason we are not walking in our purpose. We blame the government. We blame other races. We blame our parents. We blame our children. We blame the disloyal friend or the unfaithful spouse. We blame our boss for overlooking us. We blame our parents for never believing in us. I hate to burst your bubble; but none of these things are your real enemy. None of these things have any power over your life. Even your true enemy must submit to the authority of God.

You have a purpose. There is a divine calling on your life. God has an assignment only you can fulfill and with that assignment comes a target on your back. With your assignment comes adversity. The enemy will try his best to confuse you, to make you question your call. The enemy will do all he can to distract you, discourage you and make you doubt God even called you. Many of you reading this book started out strong serving in the army of the Lord. But after a while you begin to question if what you heard was correct. The opposition grew louder, and the opportunities grew dimmer.

Just the other day an acquaintance of mine was sharing her story with me. She was feeling pretty good about how her life was headed. She had just made a major career choice and was about to relocate in a couple of weeks. As she was talking I interrupted her and asked her if she has consulted God about her decision. Her response was she didn't need to. Everything had gone so smoothly that it had to have come from God. It was just too perfect. Her response had me pause. This was a Christian woman who went to church and appeared to have an intimate relationship with God. So, what caused her to think because her decision appeared to be free of adversity it must be from God?

Two things immediately cause me to see the error in this line of thinking. Satan is the father of lies and deceit. His job is to confuse the mind. He creates illusions of peace in the temporary. He distracts us with the things of the world. Everything the enemy does is in direct contradiction with God. *Jesus said, "In this world you will have tribulation but be of good cheer I have overcome the world.*" **John 16:33** Lack of adversity is not a sign that it is God's will just as the presence of adversity does not mean the absence of God.

Psalm 23:4 says,

"Yes, though I walk through the valley of the shadow of death, I will fear no evil:"

Although I live in the valley in the midst of darkness and danger, I will not give in to my fear. I will stand in confidence on the promises of God. I am fully convinced in this state God will supply everything I need. His grace will be sufficient. Take note that there is no confidence in the psalmist himself. All his confidence is in God. God is the light he is able to find amid darkness. This light provides for him comfort and joy. Why wouldn't the psalmist be confident in God. In verse one he tells us *"The Lord is my Shepherd. I shall not want."* **Psalm 23:1**

The tone of this psalm would have me believe that it was written during the latter years of his life. This psalm depicts an intimate relationship between the psalmist and the Shepherd. There is a calm and a confidence in each verse. There is experience in each statement. Often when I recite this psalm I picture David sitting in a circle with his family saying, "Let me tell you a few things about God."

The God of Israel, Yahweh, is my Shepherd." He cares about my safety and my welfare. There is nothing that I need He does not provide for me.

Now may the God of peace who brought again from the dead our Lord Jesus, the great shepherd of the sheep, by the blood of the eternal covenant, [21]equip you with everything good that you may do his will, working in us that which is pleasing in his sight, through

Jesus Christ, to whom be glory forever and ever. Amen. **Hebrews 13:20-21**

For the LORD God is a sun and shield; the LORD bestows favor and honor. No good thing does he withhold from those who walk uprightly. **Psalm 84:11**

He who did not spare his own Son but gave him up for us all, how will he not also with him graciously give us all things? **Romans 8:32**

He makes me lie down in green pastures.

I am a city girl with glimpses of the country. That means I went to the country when my parents made me. So, I don't know anything about sheepherding. I had to do a little research. Much to my surprise green pastures don't just happen they are caused. Most of the land the sheep graze in is rocky and barren due to extensive heat and lack of rain. Before they are led to greener pastures, the shepherd has cleared the rocks, tilled the soil, planted the seed, and watered the ground in preparation for the sheep's arrival. There is great care given by the shepherd to ensure the sheep have everything they need.

This is how we should picture how God provides for us. There is great thought given by God for our provision. It doesn't just happen. God knows us. **Psalm 139:13-16** says,

"You made my whole being; you formed me in my mother's body. [14] I praise you because you made me in an amazing and wonderful way. What you have done is wonderful. I know this very well. [15] You saw my bones being formed as I took shape in my mother's body. When I was put together there, [16] you saw my body as it was formed. All the days planned for me were written in your book before I was one day old."

There is no detail about you or I that is hidden from God. God in His Omniscience already sees down the road and knows exactly what you will need. I remember one Friday night on my way home from the church. I exited the highway and suddenly, my car would not accelerate past fifteen miles per hour. I looked at my temperature gauge and noticed it had moved past the halfway mark and was nearing hot. I called a friend who said pull over, let the car cool down and then you should be able to make it home. I did just that and made it home. The next morning there was a funeral of an associate minister of our church. I wanted to go and support the family and my pastor. I wasn't sure what my car was going to do but I was determined to go. I prayed and asked God to let me make it to the funeral and back home. I made it all the way to the funeral without the car running hot. As I got in my car to go home I decided to take a different route. Everything was looking good. God had answered my prayer. As I was driving, just about five minutes from my home, my car started dinging, the dashboard read 'car overheating'. My car died.

Ramona's instinct is to panic and go into full blown anxiety attack. I turned on my hazard lights and put my head down on the steering ready to scream at God. At that moment I looked up and saw a sign that said Kennedy Tire and Auto Repair Shop almost right across the street from where my car stopped. I picked up my phone and asked Siri for the number. I called them and they came and pulled my car to their shop. The master technician looked at it and told me I needed a new thermostat and a hose replaced. He then told me the price. I didn't have it, but my earthly angel did. I sat in the waiting room that day at peace. The LORD, my Shepherd had led me to greener pastures. I never go that way home. God, however, knew my car would break down and set up provision for me.

This was just one of the many times in my life God has done this for me. Over the years green pastures have represented so many different things. They have represented rest and refreshment, safety and security, peace and provision. There were times when I had to be led kicking and screaming because I was too stupid to let God guide me to greener pastures. These were the times God allowed me to experience a layoff, a health crisis, and yes even death. It still amazes me when I reflect on my life how God had already set things up where I would be taken care of. That is who God is though. He is the One who took over total management of our well-being when we turned our lives over to Him. Satan was the original property owner. On the day we gave our heart to God and died to self our debt with Satan was cancelled. God became our new manager and our every need fell under His care. His call to us was fulfillment of the promise Jesus made in **Matthew 11:28** which says, *"Come to Me, all who labor and are heavy lade, and I will give you rest."*

God desires to be more than our crisis manager. He wants to be our owner where we trust Him with the safety and welfare of our very lives. The rest God gives us is not always away from the daily activities and cares of life, but rest while in those activities. If we truly need it, we must know God will provide it. We also must trust there arc things we may not know that we need and learn to receive those things readily without bucking against the gentle nudging of the rod.

The psalmist goes on to say the Shepherd leads me beside still waters. I remember reading this for an assignment in college and wondering what is the significance behind the term still waters?

The word still is synonymous with stagnant. Stagnant waters are often polluted with everything imaginable. Discarded cans, dirty diapers, insects, parasites, and bacteria. Still waters sounded more dangerous than refreshing. Then I learned a better translation of the word still was calming. The Shepherd leads me beside calming waters.

Picture this (in my Sophia Patrillo voice from the sitcom Golden Girls), a bubbling stream that is beautiful to the eyes, cool to the touch, and refreshing to the tongue. Whether after traveling in the intense heat or after a period of rest, the shepherd leads the sheep to calming waters. The shepherd must lead the sheep to calm waters lest the sheep wander off to rivers with rushing water where there is a danger of being carried away. The sound of the waters draws the sheep their direction. However, when the sheep attempt to drink from the water their swift and violent streams can carry the sheep down the stream into even more torrential waters.

I have lived with depression and anxiety for over thirty years. I was diagnosed as a teenager. There have been times over these thirty years when my anxiety attacks were so severe I thought I was having a heart attack. One of the techniques I was taught to help me through these attacks was proper breathing. When I feel an attack coming on and even in the middle of a full-blown attack there are three steps. The first step is to breath in a long, slow breath through my nose. The second step is to hold it for a few seconds. The third step is to exhale slowly from my mouth. Usually I repeat this process about ten times. About the fifth or sixth time my breathing has started to return to normal. By the tenth time it is normal.

Calming waters symbolize for me the Holy Spirit. In moments of crisis the Holy Spirit comes in and speaks to my heart, calming my mind. It is the very Word of God that He calls to my remembrance that I may find calm in the midst of chaos and peace in the very peril of persecution and problems. While the Holy Spirit is always with me, it is during those moments of crisis, when I am tempted to be carried away by fear or the temptations of the world, I am led to still waters.

When I am experiencing fear, I am reminded *"For God gave us not a spirit of fear but of power and love and self-control."* **2 Timothy 1:7**

When I am tempted, I am reminded *"No temptation has overtaken you that is not common to man. God is faithful, and he will not let you be tempted beyond your ability, but with the temptation he will also provide the way of escape, that you may be able to endure it.* **I Corinthians 10:13**

When I am overwhelmed by the daily cares of life, I am reminded, **"But they who wait for the Lord shall renew their strength; they shall mount up with wings like eagles; they shall run and not be weary; they shall walk and not faint."** **Isaiah 40:31**

Ever been sitting somewhere and the enemy invades your mind? Instead of trusting the Lord with all your heart and leaning not on your own understanding, you find yourself thinking the worst possible outcome. I have. Therefore, it is so important to surrender totally to the care of the Shepherd. Still waters run deep. There is never any fear of dying of thirst. At the very moment when we need to be reminded of God's presence and His love for us, we are led.

The Shepherd is responsible for the total welfare of the sheep. He provides for the sheep green grass to graze on, still waters to drink from which have to do with the physical needs of the sheep. David then makes a shift to the spiritual needs of the sheep in verse 3 when he says, *"He restores my soul."* Sheep have a natural tendency to stray and have no idea how to find their way back. In fact, when one sheep strays others tend to follow. The shepherd could just leave the sheep out there lost and allow it to get swallowed up by a lion or remaining defenseless at the throws of nature, but he does not. He goes out, finds the sheep and brings the sheep safely back to the fold. If any injuries occurred while the sheep was away from the fold, the shepherd binds up its wounds and continues to care for the sheep.

There are times when we find ourselves exhausted, weary, and sad. Life has taken its toll on us. The periods of rest are shorter. The trial is longer. For a while we can go on as if everything is okay. Eventually our weariness moves from the inside to the outside. Our tears are uncontrollable. Our eyes grow dimmer. It was easy at first to believe the situation would change. God would answer the prayer. One morning you wake up and the situation is still the same and you are tempted to move away from what you know God says and take the matter into your own hands. The time has come to try out your own solution. You stray away from the protection of the shepherd. But do you really?

Even in times when our faith waivers and we wander away from what God says, God is still right there. His eyes are on us. His word tells us in **Psalm 139:7-12**,

"Where shall I go from your Spirit?

Or where shall I flee from your presence?

[8] If I ascend to heaven, you are there!

If I make my bed in Sheol, you are there!

⁹ If I take the wings of the morning

    and dwell in the uttermost parts of the sea,

¹⁰ even there your hand shall lead me,

    and your right hand shall hold me.

¹¹ If I say, "Surely the darkness shall cover me,

    and the light about me be night,"

¹² even the darkness is not dark to you;

    the night is bright as the day,

    for darkness is as light with you."

Yes, He will allow us to wander away, but His eyes are always on us. There is nowhere we can go from the presence of God. Although we may not feel His presence, He is always right there. He has a plan. We need to follow it. The plan includes provision for our every need. It leads us on to the path of righteousness for His name sake. As humans we want what is comfortable. Familiarity breeds comfort. Comfort tends to lead to complacency. I don't know too many people, including myself, who say, "Lord make me uncomfortable." If we are to be changed under the power of the Word of God, we must be made uncomfortable. We must allow the Word through the conviction of the Holy Spirit to change us. To draw us closer to God. To transform us into the likeness of His Son. To allow the Holy Spirit to guide our steps daily.

If all we have is mere exposure to the Word of God, it will not have its proper effect on us. What is meant by just a mere effect? This is when we occasionally read the Bible. We hear the Word of God on Sunday morning during worship service, but we don't attend Bible Study. It is our routine. We feel accomplished. We can tell God we spent time with Him this week. We may be able to pull from something the preacher said during the week to help get us through, but that's it. Life is good. I am a Christian.

It amazes me how much we say we want a better life. However, when we get right down to it we really don't want to do what it takes to get to the better life God promised us. We only want it if it is free from adversity. We only want it if it is along the easiest path with no detours, twist or turns.

Psychology Today did a study on the mere exposure effect. The results were fascinating. It was found that *"each of us can literally double or triple the amount of enjoyment we derive from life by doubling or tripling the stimuli to which we familiarize ourselves."* The premise behind this is more exposure, greater enjoyment.

I often say people don't read the Word of God more because they don't understand the treasure it holds. It is a chore rather than the pathway to an enhanced life, one filled with joy and peace. I find myself often reading the Word of God and having to stop and just say Thank you God! There is one thing I stand by and that is the Bible is more than words on a page or a historical book about things that may or may not have happened. It is God speaking. His word has life and gives life. His words have power and promote progress. The more you read the Word of God and it becomes a part of your very soul the more you will be at peace. Every single word in the Bible is good for you.

We are programmed to initially reject change. That is just the way we are set up. Let the doctor tell you that for you to be healthy you must change your eating habits. Your favorite food is fried chicken. You love soda pop. You will reject the change just so long as it appears you're getting by. You'll convince yourself the doctor didn't know what he or she was talking about. Until one day you find yourself in the emergency room with an extended hospital stay where you are forced to eat the very things you could have eaten on your own. The doctor was not trying to hurt you. The doctor was trying to lead you to a healthier lifestyle.

Righteousness is that healthier lifestyle for the believer. As newborn babes in Christ we may reject the things the Bible is telling us to do. The more familiar we become with the Word of God the more we come to enjoy it because it has proven itself to be reliable. We reach God's standard of righteousness when every attitude, every behavior and every word fall in step with what God would do. It is perfection.

Because I am biblically astute I understand perfection will not be achieved on this side of glory. We should still be striving towards perfection by surrendering our lives over to the hands of the potter who is able to take broken clay pots and shape them into something even more beautiful than it was to begin with.

Christians should be motivated to change. Instead of approaching change with hesitation, approach it with awe and wonder about what God is doing in your life. Hold fast to the promise that *God makes all things beautiful in His time.* **Ecclesiastes 3:11** Remember His Word says that **"…he who began a good work in you will bring it to completion at the day of Jesus Christ." Philippians 1:6**

Even when we walk through the valley of the shadow of death, we don't have to fear the evil that lies in wait because God is with us. The picture here is not of someone walking through a graveyard. It is the picture of one walking through life with dangers lurking on every hand. The presence of God gives us the ability to meet our tests and trials head on. The presence of God says although the devil is prowling around like a roaring lion seeking someone to devour, I'm ready for Him. I know who my enemy is. I understand that *"the weapons of our warfare are not of the flesh but have divine power to destroy strongholds. We destroy arguments and every lofty opinion raised against the knowledge of God, and take every thought captive to obey Christ, being ready to punish every disobedience, when your obedience is complete."* **II Corinthians 10:4-6**

God's path to righteousness may lead us into places where there appears to be no light, where darkness prevails. We must, however remember always that light is with us. We must look to Jesus who is the author and finisher of our faith. We can weather the storm because God is with us. God will be our guide.

The first time I ever flown in a plane I was terrified. Up to this point I drove everywhere I wanted to go. I would tell people I liked to drive, and to some extent I did. The truth was I was afraid of flying. A situation arose where I needed to get somewhere quickly, and the quickest route was to fly. I could have drove but that would have taken me two days if I pulled over to rest. So, I bit the bullet, faced my fears and purchased my first plane ticket. The day before the flight I called my doctor to request a refill for my anxiety medication. I was anticipating a panic attack.

I arrived at the airport, checked my bags, went through airport security and had a seat at the departure gate. I must have looked terrified. The next thing I knew someone in a pilot's uniform was sitting beside me. He asked me if it was my first time flying. I told him yes. He then began to run down his resume. He told me about his training, all his practice flights before obtaining his license to fly a commercial plane. He then told me how long he had been flying and all the different places he had been. He had not just flown domestic flights, he had also flown internationally. I was impressed. He said goodbye and before too long it was time to board the plane. I said a little prayer, scanned my ticket and boarded the plane. I buckled my seatbelt and soon we were in the air.

Something happened to me after talking to the pilot. I wasn't as afraid anymore. I felt better knowing more about the person who was flying the plane. I never had an anxiety attack. In fact, I didn't even take my medicine. I forgot. I even fell asleep on the plane. My fear of flying subsided because I knew the pilot.

Every day we are going to face danger. We need not fear because God is with us. God has a very impressive resume. God created the heavens and the earth. God delivered two million people from slavery. He then kept them safe as they journeyed through the desert. He walked with this same group of people as they conquered the Promised Land. One particular instance they didn't have to fight. All they did was march and shout.

An old man stood up to a king knowing He would be thrown into a lion's den and because of his faith God closed the very jaws of the lions. Three young boys in foreign territory also stood up to the king because they would not bow before him and were thrown into a fiery furnace. God shielded them from the fire and they didn't even smell like smoke. He turned water into wine, gave sight to the blind, made a lame man walk, multiplied a sack lunch, and resurrected the dead. And you still don't trust Him? Who else would you want with you in the throes of danger? David had his own testimony. With God, he killed a lion and a bear, defeated Goliath, escaped the plot of Saul to kill him. What's your story? How has God protected you from danger? We don't need to fear evil while living in the valley. *"Wait for the LORD; be strong, and let your heart take courage; wait for the LORD!"* **Psalm 27:14** We have no reason to fear the arrows that flieth by day nor the pestilence that walketh in darkness. We have no fear of the present nor of things to come. God walks with us.

I was privileged to hold my daddy's hand when he breathed his last breath. The day before I was upset with him because he told me to go home and be with his granddaughters instead of coming to see him. I did as I was told because he was still daddy. I went home but I never went to bed. I sat in my favorite chair with the ottoman and did nothing. When the phone rang early that morning, I didn't even say hello. I said, "I'm on my way." I got in my car and broke every law known to man to get to that hospital on the other side of town. I arrived and my cousin was there. My youngest sibling also arrived. I held his hand. It was still warm. He couldn't speak. Yet if he could I believe he would have said "I'm not afraid."

Later, we learned from one of the nurses just a few hours before he passed away he told her he was getting ready to go home. She teased him and said not until we get these vitals regulated. He told her not to my daughter's house. It made my heart happy to hear that. My daddy got it. My siblings and I could only travel with him so far. He knew God was with him. He had no fear of what was awaiting him on the other side. I cannot tell you what is waiting on the other side of your situation. I can tell you that you have no reason to fear no matter how dark it may get.

Principle #6

Blessings are still obtainable in the valley and guess what it has nothing to do with you.

Some of the most beautiful mountains in the world are the Blue Ridge Mountains. They are known for having a blush color when seen from a distance. Many people often wonder why they are called the Blue Ridge Mountains. It is because of the trees. A substance called isoprene is released into the atmosphere giving them the illusion of a blue color. Scattered throughout the internet are pictures of individuals standing top of various peaks in the mountains. When we see these pictures, they have smiles on their faces and we assume the journey was short and sweet. We never stop to think of what the individual had to go through to get there.

There is a distinct difference between an immature and mature Christian. It has nothing to do with age or time spent in the church. It has everything to do with time spent with God. One of the ways you can tell the difference between an immature and a mature Christian is by his or her prayer life. What is on the list? An immature Christian prays more selfish prayers and the request tend to lean toward the tangible. A mature Christian spends more time in intercessory prayer and prays for the intangible things to become permanent fixtures in their lives no matter what avenue it takes to get there.

An immature Christian will look at the success of another person and pray God bless them the same way. A mature Christian understands with great blessings come great burdens and has learned they only want what God wants for them. I understand this though. It does appear the world is winning and our enemies are prospering. The Christian is struggling while the non-Christian appears to have much success. We see more of their mountaintops and it looks good.

I John 2:16 says, *"For all that is in the world—the desires of the flesh and the desires of the eyes and pride in possessions—is not from the Father but is from the world."*

God wants us to be blessed. He just wants us to understand that our most valuable blessings are not always material. He also wants us to understand you cannot earn the blessings of God. It has absolutely nothing to do with you being good enough.

Let me start right off the bat and tell you that you will never be good enough. I know this goes against what some of you believe but if you really take an honest look at your life you will see that you have been trying maybe without knowing to be good enough. After all it is what the world teaches us. In our education system the good students are the A & B students while C is average and D & F students are bad. On the job if you want to be promoted you must be better

You will never be good enough! than someone else in the office. Women we seek the love of a man, so we try to be pretty enough or sexy enough. We are either trying to be enough to get a man or keep our man's attention. Men want the attention of that special woman and you find yourself trying to make enough money to prove yourself to her or you're even in the gym trying to get that body that will make her want you. Children want to earn their parents love by trying to be good enough. Parents try to earn the love of their children through buying them more things, trying to be good enough. Even in the church we try to be good enough to get our name called on Sunday morning, that's why we get mad when someone else's name is called, or our name is left off the program.

We live our lives under the pressure of trying to be good enough for people and it spills over into our Christian walk and we find ourselves trying to be good enough for God. We equate His blessings with our behavior. Some of us will never be A or B students. Many of us have gotten passed over for that promotion after spending all our time trying to do everything right. You even bought gifts for your boss. Ladies you don't understand why every man you meet cheats on you or just doesn't love you enough. You're a good woman. Men you don't understand why the man you know is dogging out his woman and gets the girl every time while you lose by trying to be a gentleman. And every time someone tells us we are not good enough or shows us that we are not good enough we become crushed and broken. The funny thing is it doesn't stop us the next time around from trying to be good enough again. And when it comes to our relationship with God when we don't receive the things we have prayed for we think it is because He doesn't love us, or we are just not good enough.

The Bible tells us in **Ephesians 2:8-9** *"For by grace we are saved, through faith. It is a gift of God not of works, lest any man should boast."*

I love what Eugene Peterson says in the Message Bible.
"Saving is all his idea, and all his work. All we do is trust him enough to let him do it. It's God's gift from start to finish! We don't play the major role. If we did, we'd probably go around bragging that we'd done the whole thing! No, we neither make nor save ourselves."

There are three words Paul uses here that breed familiarity with most of us. Grace. Saved. Faith.

When we hear these three words we close our ears because we think we already know what is going to come next. There is much danger in familiarity of God's Word with any Christian. As we are growing, the Word of God should take on new application to our lives. Notice I didn't say new meaning I said new application. So very briefly I want to look at these new testament words.

In this verse we find man's **desperate request**...our need to be saved.

Ephesians 2:1 speaks of us being *"dead in our trespasses and sins."* before we came to know Christ we were in danger. Danger of dying a horrible death. We were lost and drifting slowly down a horrible path to a bottomless pit. We were children of Satan. And I understand everyone doesn't really understand that. There are many people who say my life was okay before I got saved. It really wasn't. Salvation delivered you from an impending peril you can't even imagine and healed you from an infection that would have caused your very death – the infection was sin. Too many of us take our very salvation for granted. Picture this. Imagine a shepherd out looking for one of his wandering sheep and when he finds it, the sheep is in the jaws of a lion or the claws of a bear and then he pulls the sheep right from the danger. That is what God did for each of us when he saved us. He saved us from the very claws of Satan. And get this, God didn't just rescue us from the dangers lurking all around us, He delivered us from our very nature, that which lies within every one of us. I know you think you are a pretty good person and you try to show that good side to everyone. However, I know better. I know there is something, that one thing that can make the people you know go, Is that you? Go ahead and fill in the blank with you name because I know I'm right.

God didn't save us and then say Poof and pop us into heaven. He saved us to use us as instruments to bring others to Him. Salvation didn't just provide for us a pardon, but it also provided favor, blessedness and ultimately eternal life. Our problem is we don't walk in that favor. We don't readily receive that blessedness. Our focus is on our own happiness and our own comfort. Our focus is more on pleasing man than pleasing God. **Galatians 2:20** *"I have been crucified with Christ. My ego is no longer central. It is no longer important that I appear righteous before you or have your good opinion, and I am no longer driven to impress God. Christ lives in me. The life you see me living is not "mine," but it is lived by faith in the Son of God, who loved me and gave himself for me."* (MSG) It is no longer about us.

So why do we keep going back to that rule-keeping mentality? Why is it we are so focused on pleasing people or even living under the pressure of man-made religious rules? When we go back to rule-keeping, people-pleasing, peer-pressured religion mentality, we reject, abandon, and turn our backs on God's grace. If we could have just been good enough then, Christ died for nothing.

There are times I think about the sacrifice Jesus made on the cross and I am overwhelmed, especially because I know me. Sometimes I am not a good person. Sometimes I am mean and hateful, unforgiving and not compassionate. And yet, He died knowing the month, day, year and time I would be born. He knew every good thing I would do but that's not what shouts me about the resurrection. He knew every single bad thing I would do in the numbered days of my life and

He loved me enough to say I am going to lay down my life just for Ramona, knowing she will never be good enough. God knew we needed saving before we knew we needed saving. Do you get that? Take just five seconds and think about the sins you have committed. Heck let's be honest, even the ones you may have planned and then think about what God did to save you. We must never confuse the temporal safety and security of this world, with eternal security found in saving grace.

I understand why the unsaved are still trying to be good enough but what about the saved? You and me. Why is it we keep going back to this life of trying to be good enough? Why are we so focused on keeping laws when the fact is, we are going to break them? Now I'm not saying we shouldn't keep the law, nor should we continue in sin that grace may abound? I am saying the focus should be pleasing God in everything and fully accepting grace. Paul says for by GRACE we have been saved... We must lose the worldly thought that anything other than God will give us what we really need. Not education. Not wealth. Not a husband or a wife. Not socioeconomic status or your position in the church. You can have all those things and still not be saved.

It is my opinion too many of us take our salvation for granted. It's like the passengers on a cruise ship. As long as the sun is shining, and the ship is moving along with minimal turbulence they aren't concerned with the lifejackets. But let clouds come and rain start to fall with turbulent winds, passengers run to get to that lifejacket. Too many of us are just happy with being saved unaware of the dangers we face every single day of our lives that God saves us from. The devil knows you can't lose your salvation but that doesn't stop him from having you thinking you can. He will have you thinking he has more power than God. That God has no power to stop the storms in your life, that there is not a bigger purpose for the pain, a promise behind the problem that God can't love you if He is allowing that to happen in your life. He will have you so content with the things of this world that your relationship with God becomes secondary. He's sneaky like that.

You'll become so focused on your job that every opportunity for overtime you accept even if it means missing church or Bible study. He'll have you so wrapped up in that man or that woman because you believe that's where your happiness is coming from that everything you do to try and please them that if they say miss church or you don't need to serve in that ministry, you'll find yourself just a Sunday morning member and your relationship with God slowly fading. The devil will take the very thing you prayed and asked God for and have you more focused on that than God. You will forget all about **Matthew**

6:33 that brought the very blessing about, *"Seek first the kingdom of God and His righteousness and all these things shall be added unto you."*

One of our most valuable blessings is grace. Grace is what we receive daily while living in the valley. Grace is God's unmerited favor or God's Riches at Christ's Expense. Grace means to bend or stoop in kindness to another as a superior to an inferior. It is not just about us receiving what we do not deserve. It is about that fact that we

Grace is not just about receiving what we do not deserve. It is about receiving it when we really deserve the opposite.

receive it when we really deserve the opposite. I don't care how good you think you are. There are no levels to sin and the fact of the matter is we are all guilty as charged. We deserved death! Our deliverance from sin pours out of the heart God has for us, one filled with love. It is the action of God's infinite lovingkindness towards us. It was God's love that was the cause of Jesus' death. You don't have any claim to grace. God just gives it to you.

Think of it this way. We are saved by the grace of the Father who drew up the very plan of salvation that included a series of life events in thousands of people, successes and failures, good and bad to lead us to the knowledge that we needed a Savior and created the genealogy Jesus Christ. We are saved by the Son who accepted the assignment from His Father, God himself, wrapped himself up in the very sinful nature that we were born into, went through the most horrendous death every imaginable in order that we could receive salvation. And finally, we are being saved by the grace of the Holy Spirit who dwells inside of us and makes us aware of our need for it, applies it to us daily and keeps fresh our faith and hope in it. And grace didn't come by itself. It brought a group of blessings with it:

ELECTION

2 Timothy 1:9 *"Who saved us and called us to a holy calling, not because of our works but because of his own purpose and grace, which he gave us in Christ Jesus before the ages began,"*

REDEMPTION

Ephesians 1:7 *"In him we have redemption through his blood, the forgiveness of our trespasses, according to the riches of his grace,"*

JUSTIFICATION

Titus 3:7 *"So that being justified by his grace we might become heirs according to the hope of eternal life."*

PARDON

Isaiah 55:7 *"Let the wicked forsake his way, and the unrighteous man his thoughts; let him return to the Lord, that he may have compassion on him, and to our God, for he will abundantly pardon."*

ADOPTION

Ephesians 1:5 *"He predestined us for adoption as sons through Jesus Christ, according to the purpose of his will,"*

REGENERATION

Titus 3:5 *"He saved us, not because of works done by us in righteousness, but according to his own mercy, by the washing of regeneration and renewal of the Holy Spirit,"*

ETERNAL GLORY

I Peter 5:10 *"And after you have suffered a little while, the God of all grace, who has called* *you to his eternal glory in Christ, will himself restore, confirm, strengthen, and establish you."*

That's grace y'all, an extension of God's love. In the midst of warfare; we have God's grace. *"We are afflicted in every way, but not crushed; perplexed, but not driven to despair; persecuted, but not forsaken; struck down, but not destroyed;"* **II Corinthians 4:8-9**

As we mourn over the sin in our lives, we have God's grace. When we recall to our minds the innumerable daily shortcomings and trespasses and yet we can still shout over God's grace. *"If we confess our sins, he is faithful and just to forgive us our sins and to cleanse us from all unrighteousness"*. **I John 1:9**

Why? Because none of those things can take God's grace away from us. We didn't have a claim to it in the first place. Even the very faith that brought us to a belief in Jesus Christ did not originate from us. It was not birthed from within. It came from God above. That is why Paul adds these words in **Ephesians 2:9**, *"and not of ourselves"*. At every stage of the process of salvation it is not of ourselves. When we were saved, it had nothing to do with us. God does the drawing. **John 6:44** While we are being saved every day, it has nothing to do with you. **Psalm 138:8** And finally when we will be saved, it will still have nothing to do with you, it is all because of God. **Romans 8:18; 2 Cor. 4:17**

God doesn't bless you because of your behavior. God blesses you because of His goodness. If He chooses not to give you that dream job, house on the hill, spouse, healing, financial breakthrough, you are still blessed. If you must experience one hardship after another you are still blessed. Let that sink in. Stop trying to be good enough. Accept the gift of God and then allow Him to make you over so that you can then go on to do the good works that God created you for. Do them simply out of a heart that says, "Lord I love you and this is the way I say thank you for all that you have done for me." We were powerless to save ourselves. It was God who enlightened our understanding that led us to the foot of the cross, crying "Lord please save me." And Jesus looked down on us and said my child I have been waiting on you and welcomed us into God's family.

We waste so much valuable time trying to get out of situations. I am not saying we should not try to better ourselves or pursue our dreams. I am saying we should be grateful for where we are. I wasn't born with a silver spoon in my mouth. We didn't have a lot. However, I witnessed my parents doing everything they could to take care of us in moments of utilities being turned off and there barely any food in the house. My siblings and I didn't complain. In fact, those times created some of my fondest memories. Fires in the fireplace and roasting hotdogs on wire hangers. Those times drew our family closer. Since the valley is where we will spend most of our time, why not enjoy it. Why not use the time getting to know God better?

We spend most of our lives trying to be good enough for people who are fickle at best. One day they love you and the next day they don't. They are loyal to you until somebody better comes along to serve their needs. On your job you are valuable until that next bright young star comes along who will accept less money to do your same job and yet you spend more time devoted to the job than God. I will never forget the day a man asked me to stop doing what I did for the Lord to spend more time with him. That was the craziest thing I ever heard. What was my response? "I'm sorry I can't do that, you didn't die for me."

Yes, God does want some things from us. With salvation comes responsibility. He is not, however, holding salvation over our heads saying do this or I will take back my salvation. He is not even saying to do this and you need to figure out how on your own. Every good and perfect gift comes from above and He equips those He calls. There are blessings even in the valley. Here are just a few.

Therefore, I tell you, do not be anxious about your life, what you will eat or what you will drink, nor about your body, what you will put on. Is not life more than food, and the body more than clothing? Look at the birds of the air: they neither sow nor reap nor gather into barns, and yet your heavenly Father feeds them. Are you not of more value than they? And which of you by being anxious can add a single hour to his span of life? And why are you anxious about clothing? Consider the lilies of the field, how they grow: they neither toil nor spin, yet I tell you, even Solomon in all his glory was not arrayed like one of these. ... **Matthew 6:25-34**

And God is able to make all grace abound to you, so that having all sufficiency in all things at all times, you may abound in every good work. **II Corinthians 9:8**

For he satisfies the thirsty and fills the hungry with good things. **Psalm 107:9**

"The LORD is my rock and my fortress and my deliverer, my God, my rock, in whom I take refuge, my shield, and the horn of my salvation, my stronghold and my refuge, my savior; you save me from violence. **II Samuel 22:2-3**

"Though I walk in the midst of trouble, you preserve my life; you stretch out your hand against the wrath of my enemies, and your right hand delivers me." **Psalm 138: 7**

God did the work to save you and He will continue to do the work to keep you.

One day you gave God your life. My question to you is does He still have it today? I am not asking are you still saved that would contradict the very Bible I teach from, the foundation for everything I say. I am asking is He in first place? In your home? On your job? In your relationships? As you go throughout your day are you continuously plugged in to Him so that you can receive Emergency broadcast?

One Saturday morning, I was fast asleep when at 4:58 my phone started making this horrendous sound. I almost chunked it. When I looked at it I realized I had received an amber alert. A young mother and her child had gone missing. The reason I received the message is because I have my phone set to receive notifications of emergencies in my state. It doesn't matter if I'm sleep or awake, the time of day or night, where I am or who I am with if there is something I need to be made aware of my phone is going to notify me. It's the same way with the people I love, they have a different ring tone and text tone than all the rest of my contacts. Why? Because they are important to me. No matter where I am, who I'm with or what I am doing I answer their call or message.

This is exactly how God should be in our lives. He should be in first place. Because of our relationship with Him we should always be connected to receive whatever message He has for us. Sometimes it's a message asking you to do something. Sometimes it is God trying to give you something you need right at that moment. If you are not tuned in you will miss what he has for you.

Today my friends I want to leave you with this. It is okay that you are not good enough. Stop beating yourself up over that broken relationship that you may still be in or maybe you left. Stop fighting so hard to make that person like you that it causes you to stop being true to the God you serve. Stop working so hard for that promotion that you've become unethical in your actions. And most importantly, stop trying to earn God's blessings.

Stop trying to earn God's blessings ....

God didn't save you because you were good enough. He saved you because He loved you and still loves you. He is not sustaining you because of what you are doing?

[35] *"What can separate you from the love of God? Shall tribulation, or distress, or*

persecution, or famine, or nakedness, or danger, or sword? Paul goes on to say, [38] "For I am sure (or I am convinced – the KJV I memorized as a child) that neither death nor life, nor angels nor rulers, nor things present nor things to come, nor powers, 39 nor height nor depth, nor anything else in all creation, will be able to separate us from the love of God in Christ Jesus our Lord." Romans 8:35; 38-39

Principle #7

Climbing requires you to find balance between your movements and your mind.

We spend all are lives walking upright on horizontal pavements. Streets and sidewalks. Trails and tracks. But when the time comes to climb a mountain we learn to use parts of our body we never really had to use before in new ways. We don't need our arms for walking. We do, however need them for climbing. Climbing requires us to find balance between our movements and our mind.

In this chapter we will discuss two of my favorite verses. The first verse is about movement. **Acts 17:28a** says, *for* **"'In him we live and move and have our being'**... Better translated as *we live,* *and are moved, and are...* This verse covers every aspect of the human being from the physical to the emotional, to the will and the mind of man. It steps beyond the Omnipresence of God to helping us to understand that every act, emotion, and thought comes from God. God created you and it is only by Him that you will be sustained. Without God we have no life, no activity of our limbs, no existence.

So why is it we try to go through life without Him. We are good in the beginning when we pray for God to open the door, to show us favor. He sets us out on the right path and as we start up the mountain, we forget about Him. We begin to think more highly of ourselves or the people who are mere conduits of blessing from God. As my Pastor always says, "Why are you praising the resource and not The Source?"

The Bible tells us that *'every good and perfect gift comes from above'*. **James 1:17a**

The above James speaks of is not some cosmic universe or some higher being. The above that James speaks about is God, *'the Father of lights, with whom there is no variation or shadow due to change'*. **James 1:17b**

While climbing a mountain your steps must be in sync. Climbing requires you to use your hands and your feet to move upward and surmount a steep obstacle, boulders, cliffs, and the mountain wall. Experienced climbers teach novice climbers you must be tied to an anchor. Climbing is dangerous. One must do everything you can to mitigate the effects of gravity and falling. Without a good anchor, accidents are bound to happen. And usually the accident is the fault of the climber.

The Bible tells us without God we can do nothing. Our steps must be in sync with Him. One of my favorite songs is "Order my Steps in your Word." A song that should be our daily prayer. **Psalm 119:33-35** says, *"Teach me, O Lord, the way of your statutes; and I will keep it to the end. Give me understanding, that I may keep your law and observe it with my whole heart. Lead me in the path of your commandments, for I delight in it."* **Psalm 119:133** says, **"Order my steps in thy word; and let not any iniquity have dominion over me." (KJV) ESV says, "keep steady my steps…"** We have the anchor. The question becomes do we use it?

Our missteps and our inability to climb over boulders and obstacles along our path is because we are not tied to the right anchor. There is a whole lot of stuff we just will not do if we have the Word of God hidden in our hearts so that we won't sin against God. **Psalm 119:9** says, *"How can a man keep his way pure? By guarding it according to your Word."*

I mentioned in the beginning one of my most treasured possessions is my daddy's Bible. Another possession I treasure is a Christmas gift given to me by one of my best friends, Jamila Woodard. It is a handmade book of God's promises over my life with my name added to each of one them. I also have a journal with verses I have written down that serves as that two-edged sword, some comfort and some cut. Anyone who has ever attended a Sunday School class or a Christian Education class I have taught heard me stress how important it is to have a Scripture treasure chest, full of nuggets from the Bible that you have hidden in your heart that you don't need to call mama or grandma for, access google or even pull out your Bible.

In 1995 I gave birth to my firstborn son, Khalil Maliq Franklin. I became pregnant with Khalil out of wedlock while attending Oklahoma State University in Stillwater, Oklahoma. Go Pokes! Because of my pregnancy I had to drop out of school, move back to Oklahoma City and be a parent. I got a one-bedroom apartment in North Oklahoma City and found me a job. In college any money I received was mine. I was on full scholarship. I did not have any one depending on me. Now I did. Every morning when I woke up I had two beautiful brown eyes staring at me, depending on me for food, clothing and shelter. I remember receiving my first check and thinking what am I supposed to do with that. I have to pay rent, utilities, a car note, and buy food. It wasn't nearly enough and every month I struggled.

I remember one morning driving down the Broadway Extension on my way downtown to work and having a mental breakdown. It was just too much. I begin to cry. I could barely see the road. I was raised in the church. I also had parents who believed in memorizing Scripture. My siblings and I didn't have to just learn verses, we had to learn entire chapters of the Bible. I never got upset with my parents for making us do it. I just didn't see the point. On this day it all made sense.

As I continued to cry, one of the chapters we had to memorize came to mind. I begin to say the words out loud. My mother believed you should make the Word personal. So, I began to say:

I am dwelling in the Secret Place of the Most High. I am abiding under the shadow of the Almighty. I will say of the Lord He is my refuge and my fortress. My God in whom I am trusting. Surely, He has delivered me from the snare of the fowler and the noisome pestilence. He had covered me with His feathers and under His wings I am trusting. His truth is my shield and buckler. I will not be afraid of the terror by night nor the arrow that flieth by day. Nor the pestilence that walketh by night; nor the destruction that wasteth at noonday. A thousand shall fall at my side and ten thousand at my right hand but it will not come near me. Only with my eyes will I behold and see the reward of the wicked. Because I have set my love upon Him, He will deliver me. He will set me on high because I have known His name. I will call upon Him and He will answer me. He will deliver me and honor me. With long life will He satisfy me and show me His salvation. (author's paraphrase, **Psalm 91**)

After reciting those verses, a peace came over me like never before. I instantly knew everything was going to be okay. I didn't have to worry. God would take care of me and my son. I picked up the phone and called my mother and told her thank you. I thank God because just when I needed my anchor, He was right there. We may try to tie ourselves to many things; but as the old hymn says, *'we should be very sure our anchor holds and grips a solid rock. That rock is Jesus. He's the only One'*.

The second verse I want to discuss is **Philippians 4:8.**

"Finally, brothers, whatever is true, whatever is honorable, whatever is just, whatever is pure, whatever is lovely, whatever is commendable, if there is any excellence, if there is anything worthy of praise, think about these things."

Remember I said mountain climbing requires us to find the balance between our movements and our mind. Not only will there be physical obstacles there will also be mental demons you have to fight. Mountain climbing has many benefits. All too often we never see them because we give up before we get there. However, for every mountain God helps us climb over there are blessings we receive. Too often, the minute we see an obstacle we are ready to turn back around and stop climbing. Therefore, we must be mentally prepared. We must set our minds on things above. We must be ready to combat the boulder with the Word of God.

When Paul wrote these words in the book of Philippians he was referring to the Word of God. What else can you think of that is always honest, always pure, always just, always of good report, excellent and praiseworthy. Personally, I can't think of anything or anyone that always has these characteristics. However, the Word of God does. **John 1:1** says, ***"In the beginning was the Word and the Word was with God and the Word was God."*** Essentially Paul is telling us to have God-thoughts. When everything around us looks impossible, when that boulder in your life seems insurmountable, think on these things.

What are some of the boulders of life we will encounter?

The Boulder of Fear

2Timothy 1:7 *for God gave us a spirit not of fear but of power and love and self-control.*

The Boulder of Weakness:

II Corinthians 12:9 *But he said to me, "My grace is sufficient for you, for my power is made perfect in weakness." Therefore, I will boast all the more gladly of my weaknesses, so that the power of Christ may rest upon me.*

The Boulder of Low Self-Esteem

Psalm 139:13-14 *For you formed my inward parts; you knitted me together in my mother's womb.* [14] *I praise you, for I am fearfully and wonderfully made. Wonderful are your works; my soul knows it very well.*

The Boulder of Discouragement

John 16:33 *I have said these things to you, that in me you may have peace. In the world you will have tribulation. But take heart; I have overcome the world."*

The Boulder of Depression

Isaiah 41:10 *Fear not, for I am with you; be not dismayed, for I am your God; I will strengthen you, I will help you, I will uphold you with my righteous right hand.*

The Boulder of Doubt

I John 5:14-15 [14] *And this is the confidence that we have toward him, that if we ask anything according to his will he hears us.* [15] *And if we know that he hears us in whatever we ask, we know that we have the requests that we have asked of him.*

When I was young I was diagnosed with depression. Because I grew up in a Christian home, we believed depression was of the devil and you could pray it away. Even today when I speak about my battle I will have people to tell me I must not be praying enough or living right. Real Christians can't be depressed. These responses used to sink me further into my depression because I believed the church was a place I should be able to seek refuge from what was ailing me. It was very difficult for me to discover that my transparency caused me to be judged. So, I learned how to hide my sickness. Keep the smile showing. Never let them see me sweat.

As I got older and became more educated about my illness I realized there were ways for me to live a better life through medication and counseling. I began to receive regular counseling and started taking medication. I started feeling better. I returned to what I knew. I started reading my Bible, praying, teaching, serving, and spending time with God. But every time I was on a steady path climbing my way upward, an obstacle showed up I would become severely depressed and begin to feel worthless and speak negativity into my life. I begin to doubt everything God had said to me and who He had called me to be. I would stop taking my medicine, wouldn't go to counseling which resulted in me trying take my own life twice.

The second time I went into the hospital part of my action plan after my release was I had to commit to taking my medication and go back to counseling. This time God led me to a Christian counselor. This counselor began by asking me if I was a Christian. I said yes. She then went on to ask me did I know what God thought about me? I said I guess. She then said, apparently you don't because you tried to take your own life and you do not realize how valuable you are to God. Honestly, I never thought about it that way. Remember I said in my introduction I was a people pleaser and I put a lot of weight on what others thought about me and for the things I had to go through so far in life I couldn't be worth much.

She opened her Bible and went to **Luke 12:6-7**. *"Are not five sparrows sold for two pennies? And not one of them is forgotten before God. [7] Why, even the hairs of your head are all numbered. Fear not; you are of more value than the sparrows."* Then she gave me a homework assignment. I had to go through the Bible and find Scriptures that said what I meant to God.

I won't tell you about every session. I will tell you in that year I discovered so much about God and even more about myself. It helped me to really bring the God of the Bible to the God of Ramona. I realized all the things God had spoken to me in my spirit over the years, He still wanted for me. I had to learn who my real enemy was. I was not my own enemy, and neither were the people who had done me wrong or I felt had held me back from what God had promised me. The truth was I was unprepared. I wasn't ready to go to the mountaintop. I was not ready to climb over that obstacle to the next phase of what God had for me. The words from the world was louder in my ears than the words of God. Something had to change.

Ephesians 6 was another chapter my parents made us learn. During this time of self-awareness, I was reminded of verse 12. *"For we do not wrestle against flesh and blood, but against the rulers, against the authorities, against the cosmic powers over this present darkness, against the spiritual forces of evil in the heavenly places."* I was also reminded of **2 Corinthians 10:4-5**. *"For the weapons of our warfare are not of the flesh but have divine power to destroy strongholds. We destroy arguments and every lofty opinion raised against the knowledge of God, and take every thought captive to obey Christ."* Bottom line of these verses was I had to stop blaming others. Which one of them was more powerful than God? Not one of them!

It's a grind climbing a mountain. If you are ill-equipped or inexperienced you will get winded, fall back, and take breaks. All these things are okay if you continue to move upward. In the beginning it appears to be fun; however, after about thirty minutes in you realize you have some work ahead of you.

You must be able to talk to yourself. Shake the devil off. Think on these things. Have God-thoughts from the beginning to the end.

What is true?

Malachi 3:6 *"For I the LORD do not change;"*

II Corinthians 1:20 *"For all the promises of God find their Yes in him. That is why it is through him that we utter our Amen to God for his glory."*

What is honorable?

Deuteronomy 7:9 *"Know therefore that the LORD your God is God, the faithful God who keeps covenant and steadfast love with those who love him and keep his commandments, to a thousand generations,"*

Psalm 89:8 "O LORD God of hosts, who is mighty as you are, O LORD, with your faithfulness all around you?"

What is just?

Isaiah 30:18 *"Therefore the LORD waits to be gracious to you, and therefore he exalts himself to show mercy to you. For the LORD is a God of justice; blessed are all those who wait for him."*

Romans 12:19 *"Beloved, never avenge yourselves, but leave it to the wrath of God, for it is written, "Vengeance is mine, I will repay, says the Lord."*

What is pure?

Matthew 24:35 *"Heaven and earth will pass away, but my words will not pass away."*

I Corinthians 6:18 *"Flee from sexual immorality. Every other sin a person commits is* *outside the body, but the sexually immoral person sins against his own body."*

What is lovely and of good report?

Psalm 145.18 "The Lord is near to all who call on him, to all who call on him in truth."

I Corinthians 2:9 *"But, as it is written, "What no eye has seen, nor ear heard, nor the heart of man imagined, what God has prepared for those who love him"*

What is excellent and praiseworthy?

Psalm 18:3 *"I call upon the LORD, who is worthy to be praised, and I am saved from my enemies."*

Psalm 138:8 *"The Lord will fulfill his purpose for me; your steadfast love, O LORD, endures forever. Do not forsake the work of your hands."*

These are just a few Scriptures you can add to your Spiritual Treasure Chest. They are guaranteed to be boulder crushers and obstacle leapers. Controlling our thoughts is more than a suggestion. It is imperative. It is critical for mountain climbing completion.

I have three teenage daughters and they hate when I control what they watch on television. They do not understand that what goes in will eventually come out. Most Christians don't understand this concept either. If seventy-five percent of our time is spent with the daily routines of life and twenty-five percent is spent on the things of God, what do you believe is going to come out of you during difficult times? Now just imagine if you began your day with time with God and all throughout your day you're talking to Him. When temptation arises, you respond with "It is written…" When doubt arises you respond with, "My God said…" When fear creeps in you respond with, "Jesus said…"

We are living in a time when our President is calling for the building of a wall to keep immigrants out of our country. My desire is not to change what you think politically. My goal here is to make you think. What if you kept a guard or built a wall around your mind and didn't allow anything to pass through that did not fall in line with your new bloodline. The one that was created by the blood Jesus shed at Calvary. The only things you allow through the gate are those things that are true, honest, just, pure, lovely, of good report, excellent and praiseworthy. Imagine how much better your life would be. Imagine being able to climb that mountain and reach the peak regardless of the obstacles you may face along the way.

Climbing requires us to find balance between our movements and our mind. We learned our movements are controlled by God and we must allow our minds to be controlled by the One who controls our movements. That is how we stay in step as we climb the mountain. We learn to only move when God says move. There is a phrase I repeat from a song played during a scene from the movie You Got Served starring Omarion and Marques Houston when they were learning one of their dance routines for competition. "When I move you move, just like that." Our success is climbing over the mountains in our life, and it is tied to listening to God and moving only when He says move. And furthermore, in those periods of stillness, building a wall around our thoughts made up of God's Word.

Principle #8

When in the valley, sometimes you have to FAITH it until you make it.

I cannot take the credit for this statement. My Pastor said it one Sunday and it stuck with me ever since. There have been many days when I have had to get up, wash my face, brush my teeth, put on my clothes and go on with my day all while feeling defeated, discouraged and depressed. Some days I would have to pull the covers from over my head and say okay "I am just going to give myself one more hour, set my alarm and just get up." And I did just that. Days in this state turned to weeks and weeks turned to months and months turned to years. Yes, I lived for years pressing my way through.

A few nights ago, I was watching my recording of the show Scandal starring Kerry Washington.

Scandal is a show about a Fixer (Washington) who is hired to help people through the situations we sometimes find ourselves in. Many people don't like the show because of Olivia's affair with Fitz (the President of the United States). However, I am not here to debate your like or dislike of the show. On this episode Olivia is teaching a course at a college. She writes on the board, "How to get away with Scandal". She then asks the question, "What is the biggest mistake one makes in a crisis?" Many answers were given and then one final answer was given that relates to our principle for this chapter. "The biggest mistake one makes is not knowing they are in a crisis." What you say!

How many times in your life have you found yourself living life as if everything is okay? You are still going to work, taking care of your family, spending time with friends, working in ministry. To the outside world all looks well. But the truth of the matter is you were dying on the inside. You didn't want to admit it at first but as time rolled on it became harder and harder to get up, to put on that fake smile, to hide the tears, to act as if you care. Even now you aren't ready to have an honest conversation with yourself about where you are. You would much rather keep up the façade than show anyone that you, yes you, don't have it all together. You don't have it all figured out.

Social media has become your hiding place. Your followers just don't know you took twenty pictures just to get the one with the smile that wouldn't cause anyone to ask questions. You don't want people to know your marriage is falling apart. You feel like a failure as a parent. You are so deep in debt that you are one step away from being homeless. You work hard every Sunday not to shed a tear because you don't want anyone asking you any questions. How do I know? I have been there myself. Remember I said it started out as a few days and then days turned to weeks and weeks turned to months and months turned to years. Yes, I said years. I lived for years in a state of 'show the world you have it all together. Never let them see you sweat'. Until one day it all came crashing down.

Now I'm sure you are wondering how this fits in with the principle of this chapter. The principle is a pun on the phrase, "Fake it till **There is a** you make it." Yes, it is. **huge** However, there is a **difference** huge difference **between** between fake and faith. **fake and** Fake is defined as **faith.** 'not genuine or counterfeit'. Faith is defined as 'the substance of things hoped for the evidence of things not seen'. When one is faking he or she is trying to deceive someone else. When one is faking it is not in hope of a better outcome. It is to cover up what is real. Deception is never a good thing.

On the other hand, the very foundation of faith is God. God is real. Faith is real. When we have faith, we have confident expectation that the situation can and will get better, not because of anything we do on our own, but because God said so in His Word. Faith is not passive. When one exercises faith, he or she is not sitting idly by wishing things to get better. Faith is persistent. Faith is you saying to your situation what God says about it. Faith is you letting God know that you believe Him.

Let's take a minute and dissect Hebrews 11:1.

"Now faith is the assurance of things hoped for, the conviction of things not seen."

First off, I want to change your thinking a little and say this verse is not a definition of faith. It describes what faith does. I want to make this clear from the beginning because many

"True Bible faith is confident obedience to God's Word despite circumstances and consequences." Warren Wiersbe

people look at faith as blind or risk-taking. It is also not superstition. Faith must be attached to the pillar on which it stands. The word of God. When we think about true faith it is having confidence in God's Word no matter what we may see with our physical eyes. Warren Wiersbe says in his book Be Confident, "True Bible faith is confident obedience to God's Word despite circumstances and consequences."

Faith is not weak. In the King James Version of this Scripture it says, "Now faith is the substance…" SUBSTANCE. What does this word mean? The word translated substance here in this text literally means, "to stand under, to support. Years ago, I was blessed to go through the process of building a home from start to finish. Once the floorplan was selected, then a lot of land had to be chosen. Only certain lots would fit the square footage of the home. The lot was selected and every day or two I would drive by to see the progress. The home was located in what was described as tornado alley in Oklahoma City, Oklahoma. One thing was very important to me was the foundation. The foundation had to be perfectly laid. The strength of my home rested in the foundation. For my home to remain above ground and upright the foundation had to be strong. In talking with the builder, I discovered the true purpose of a foundation.

1. The basic part of the foundation is to load the entire structure.

2. A good and strong foundation keeps the building standing while the forces of nature wreak havoc. Well-built foundations keep the occupants of the building safe during calamities such as earthquake, floods, strong winds etc.

3. The foundation must be built such that, it keeps the ground moisture from seeping in and weakening the structure.

So, what does this mean in relation to faith? Think about it. Faith is meant to support the load of life. You were never meant to carry the burdens of life. Yes, they would come but your shoulders were never designed to support them. The foundation of a building is designed to not just carry the weight of the building but also, it's occupants and anything they bring along with them. Wow! This fact almost made me lose my mind about faith. The foundation of faith is the Word of God. When we exercise our faith correctly it will hold us up and all the baggage we bring. In an earlier chapter I said salvation didn't cure us completely. Yes, we are saved once and for all. However, each day as we surrender to God we are being perfected. There are still things in us God is trying to remove.

We were born as children of Satan. When we confess with our mouths and believe in our hearts that God raised Jesus from the dead and we have a true encounter with Jesus, we are saved. Our baggage doesn't magically disappear. We still have some of those worldly beliefs. We still have that negative attitude. We still have some old habits that need to be broken. We may still be in that sinful relationship. We may still try to do things our own way. God says, "That's okay. Keep praying and spending time in my Word. Let the Holy Spirit do its job and help to grow your faith." Bottom line, God understands. He can handle your flaws and imperfections. He just wants you to have enough faith to give them to Him.

Not only is faith designed to support the dead weight and the live weight. Faith is designed to help the structure not to buckle from the weight of outside forces. Living in a state with tornadoes I had to be sure the foundation of the house could support the forces of nature that may occur. And even if the structure was somewhat damaged my family would be safe through rain, hell, strong winds, and yes even a tornado. Of course, the builder could not guarantee the safety of my family one hundred percent. He could, however, guarantee my home would have a sturdy and strong foundation.

What external forces have threatened to take you out? Was it depression, divorce, or maybe even death? Was it sickness, shame, or sin you have had a hard time giving up? Situations come up in our lives are many times frightening and we think unbearable. It is our nature to try and fix them ourselves instead of giving them over to God. We only do this when we are not exercising our faith. Answer these questions for me.

Can you control the chemical imbalance that causes depression and anxiety?

Can you stop the one you love from leaving you?

Are you able to stop your loved one from breathing his or her last breath?

Do you have the power to heal?

Can you undo what has already been done?

Are you able to stop sinning on your own?

Can you stop your company from closing?

Can you make that person stop lying and gossiping about you?

Can you stop your child from getting addicted to drugs or committing that crime?

I could go on and on, but I will stop there. I don't need to hear your response to know the answer to every one of those questions is No. **Jeremiah 32:27** says however, *""Behold, I am the LORD, the God of all flesh. Is anything too hard for me?"* Jesus Himself said in **Luke 18:27**, *"But he said, "What is impossible with man is possible with God."* No, you don't have the ability to do any of those things, but God does. Faith is having confidence in God's omniscience and His Omnipotence. Faith is having confidence God has the power and ability to do anything and at the same time uses that knowledge to do what is best in your life.

I know this is not an easy pill to swallow. I know even now some of you don't see the good in the divorce or understand that constant cloud of darkness you live under with depression. You haven't yet bounced back from the loss of your loved one. You still must work two jobs after losing your dream job when the company shut down. I know, and I understand. Many of you are right now unable to forgive yourself or outrun the guilt of disappointing God through your actions. You can't forgive that person that did you wrong. You still blame him or her for the reason you are struggling.

That is not the case. Everything happened in your life, God allowed. I am a domestic violence survivor. I lived many nights in fear for my life. Would I want that for myself? Absolutely not! When I went through it did I say, "Thank you God for taking me through this because I will know you better and trust you more when I come out of it." No, I thought I would die. I wasn't thinking God was taking me through it so that I would become more like Him. I didn't have faith like my dad that said even through this I am going to trust you Lord. I understand your feelings. I just know God better now. I know had He not taken me through that then I would not have the unshakeable faith I have right now. I have had people call me crazy because I just believe that God will keep His promises. I am no longer looking for comfort here on earth. I want to live a life that pleases God as I make my way to my eternal blessings. I am headed to Heaven. It is more about my permanent security than my temporary satisfaction. I am a living testimony that the faith has stood up against the external forces that tried to destroy me. I am evidence of God's Word that says, *"God is able to do what He has promised."* **Romans 4:21**

The turbulence, tests, and trials God allows in our lives cause us to grow up so after twenty years of being saved, God is not saying like Paul said in **I Corinthians 3:2,** *"I fed you with milk, not solid food, for you were not ready for it. And* *even now you are not yet ready."* By now you should be able to testify to those coming up alongside you and after you that the best thing for your life is to have faith in God. No matter what happens in your life believe what He says.

The final point I want to make about the substance of faith is faith can handle your doubts. I will never forget when my Intermediate Bible teacher said to me I shouldn't ask God questions. When I asked her why she gave me the answer most parents give their children, "Because I said so." I didn't know then what I know now and that is doubt left undealt with will lead to destruction. It

Faith can handle your doubts.

is so easy for the enemy to grab a hold of our minds. I know we would love it if we lived in a bubble where we don't see the horrible things going on in the world and even our own lives that make you think God is not there. There are those of you reading this book who are living in a situation that has gone on for years. Abuse, jobs, marriages, weekly medical treatments are just a few I can think of right off the top of my head. I don't have to know you to say your situation has caused you to doubt God. You have wanted to give up on God and say to heck with your Christian walk.

First thing I want to say to you it is okay to ask God why. It is God's Word that tells us to pray. Prayer is a conversation with God. Prayer works when you are honest about where you are so God can be God in your life. It does not work with deception or what I like to call 'empty prayers'. You know those prayers that say, "Heavenly Father I thank you for who you are. I praise Your holy name. Bless me and my family. Thank you for everything you have done in my life. Thank you for loving me and for your grace and mercy. I thank you for Jesus and Lord if you never do anything else for me, You've already done enough. In Jesus' name I pray Amen."

You pray that prayer while your life is in a state of chaos. You think God wants you to tell Him you trust Him when you really don't. I remember being in a relationship where the man said, "I'm only after one thing and that is for you to truly trust me with your heart." My response back to him was, "I trust you more than I have ever trusted anyone." It took me a while to understand he wanted so much more. That is what God is saying to each of us. He is asking for our honesty in every situation. Go ahead and tell God I don't understand. Go ahead and tell God the weight of this trial is too much for me to bear. You don't feel His love. You don't feel His presence. You are going through the motion. You are on the verge of quitting life. It is your honesty with God that opens doors to your MORE. It is your honesty with God that leads you to the treasure found in His Word that can stand up against the doubt the enemy tries to sneak into your mind.

The Word becomes your weapon against the fiery darts of the enemy.

The enemy says, "You're worthless." You say, *"I am God's workmanship, created in Christ Jesus for good works, which God prepared beforehand, that we should walk in them."* **Ephesians 2:10**

The enemy says, "See God doesn't have the power to heal you." You say, *"Many are the afflictions of the righteous, but the LORD delivers him out of them all."* **Psalm 34:19**

The enemy says, "You've messed up too many times. God doesn't love you anymore." You say, *"For I am sure that neither death nor life, nor angels nor rulers, nor things present nor things to come, nor powers, nor height nor depth, nor anything else in all creation, will be able to separate us from the love of God in Christ Jesus our Lord."* **Romans 8:39**

The enemy says, "You will always be broke." You say, *"And my God will supply every need of yours according to his riches in glory in Christ Jesus."* **Philippians 4:19** And for good measure you follow it up with, *"The Lord is my Shepherd, I shall not want."* **Psalm 23:1**

Not only does faith have substance, real faith is solid. The writer of Hebrews continues by saying "…it is the evidence of things hoped for." Most would equate the words hoped for with wishful thinking. But not so in this text. Here we are to be convinced and convicted that God will keep His Word. And the fact that we are convinced means we follow up that conviction with action.

Self-worth has always been a struggle of mine. I never wanted the spotlight because under the spotlight your imperfections are bolded. Under the spotlight people expect you to live a perfect life and when you don't you have the pressure of taking others down with you. Under the spotlight you see the nastiness of people. Under the spotlight you find out people you thought were for you are secretly hoping for and even plotting for your demise. So, for most of my life I tried to fly under the radar. I knew how messed up my life really was. I knew what most people saw was the dressed-up me. I could do my hair, put on a little makeup, wear nice clothes, say the right things, and of course always flash my signature smile when needed. I didn't however ever want to be called on or have to stand in front of people. God has a sense of humor though because the one thing I was so fearful of He gifted me with. Imagine that! (insert smile) Easter speeches. I was always given the longest ones with the most

Scriptures. School. I made straight A's and was known as the teacher's pet. Church. I taught Sunday School, led the Women's Ministry Bible Study, leader of the Young Adult in my district, and became a preacher's wife. I didn't ask for any of this. As a matter of fact, I ran from it. And I was so miserable. I knew I wasn't living my life the way God intended. Not pleasing God is not always about sin. We displease God when we don't follow His direction for our lives. Truth was, I was afraid. I was afraid I would fail. I was also afraid of mean people.

I love church. There was a period in my life when I forgot the church was made up of imperfect people on the same journey as I was. We were all there wanting God to make us better. Some surrendered to the makeover process; others did not. During this period the more God elevated me, the more I felt attacked. Truth was He was not elevating me, He was just showing up in me more. His light was shining.

When the attack came I was unable to withstand it. I buckled under the pressure. God had told me to do some things and when everything happened, I told Him no. It wasn't worth it. I didn't believe He was with me anymore. I didn't stand on His Word. I gave in to some very human emotions. God had lied to me. He sent me out to the wolves and left me unprotected. My faith waivered. I was not fully convinced of the promises I had memorized as a child. I did not possess that inward conviction that showed up outwardly. My faith was a little phony. The God I talked about had not yet become personal. I knew about Him. I believed He did all the lessons I taught from stories in the Bible. I didn't yet have my own stories that made them real.

While I thought God had left me out there with the wolves, truth is it was during those times He loved me the most. God had to get me to the place that I realized my ability had nothing to do with me. I didn't think I needed to be humbled but let your name be called enough and pride can easily sneak in. He had to show me it wasn't about who I was connected to. Even though it may not sound like it, there were people who truly loved and supported me. They were the ones who gave me the opportunities to stand. God had to break me down into a million pieces to then put me back together the right way, so my life could be used for His glory. He had to show me it wasn't about who liked me or supported me. I was called to serve an audience of One. This is why today you are reading this book. God's glory is finally more important than me. I am fully convinced *"that he who began a good work in you will bring it to completion at the day of Jesus Christ."* **Philippians 1:6** I now say like Paul said in **Acts 20:24**, *"But I do not account my life of any value nor as precious to myself, if only I may finish my course and the ministry that I received from the Lord Jesus, to testify to the gospel of the grace of God."*

In addition to the promises found in the Word of God, there are some specific things God has promised regarding your personal life. He has told some mother He was going to bring that wayward child home. He has told someone He is going to heal you of that disease. He has given someone a vision for ministry. All God is waiting on now is for your actions to catch up with your faith. "Faith it until you make it." God is doing His part, now you do yours. It is what I like to call Faith-walking.

"For we walk by faith, not by sight."
2 Corinthians 5:7

I had someone tell me once when I was complaining about a period of difficulty, "grow through it." I asked her how and she said, "keep walking." I love to hear about God delivering the children of Israel, parting the Red Sea, raining down manna, making bitter water sweet, closing the mouth of the lion and being a barrier between the fire, turning water into wine, raising Jairus' daughter, feeding the five thousand; however, reading those stories requires nothing of us. It is only through our personal journey of trust we come to know God. That place where we are not looking at God asking for anything instead we are in a total submissive stance kneeling before the Father saying, "Anything you want from me Lord I'll do. Anything you want to take me through Lord I accept, and I trust you. Sickness. Death. Unemployment. Divorce. No matter what comes my way, Lord my life is in your hands. Daily we say, have thine own way Lord. Have thine own way. Thou art the potter. I am the clay.

Mold me and make me after thy will. While I am waiting yielded and still.

Faith-walking requires SACRIFICE. At times it requires us to sacrifice our comfort or our practicality. Remember I said sometimes what God tells us to do sounds foolish to the world. It doesn't make common sense. Other times it will require us to sacrifice our comfort. God you mean you want me to go there and do what? I'm used to having everything I need at my disposal. Instead of ministry in the church you want me to start a ministry for homeless women in a shelter. You mean you want me to leave the big city and minister at a church in what town…population 500. You mean you're asking me to be the spokesperson for the wrong being spoken about my sister or brother. I don't agree with it, but I don't want to be the one to say anything about it. It really doesn't concern me.

For most of us God will never call to give up all our worldly comforts and move to a foreign country where there is no running water. He's just asking you to live for Him more than one day a week. He's asking that we trust Him enough that every time hardship comes He is not having to prove Himself over and over again. When trouble comes you say with confidence, Lord I'm not sure why this is happening, but I know that you know and there is a very good reason. Help me not to fight against your plan and help me to learn whatever it is I need to learn. I always say it's okay to doubt for a moment, just don't stay there.

Unbelief is at the root of a lot of the struggles we face. When we don't believe God, we make the mistake of thinking we can do things only God can do. And we stay stuck living a mediocre life because we are too afraid to step out on faith.

Faith is the pillar we stand on that says we can wait with confident expectation for good things

Unbelief is at the root of many of our struggles. to come to us. Not everything we want but those things that will aid in the process of us becoming more like Christ, looking more like Jesus. Holiness not happiness. It is our faith in God that will stand the test of time when everything around us looks like we're losing. It's when you can say with confidence don't look at what you see now because the final chapter hasn't been written to my story. I have God on my team.

Just look at me. I started out with a good story. Smart. Graduated top of my class. Received several offers for full scholarships to college then got pregnant. Dropped out of college. Went to work full time. Struggled as a single mom. Got married. Went through a very public scandal.

Got divorced. Went through a very dark period of life. Quit church. Quit people. Went back to church. Got married again. Got divorced. Lost my dad. Went through church hurt. Lost almost everything. Quit life. Doesn't sound like the story of a winner, does it? Doesn't sound like the story of someone who God loves. Doesn't sound like the story of someone who has the favor of God on her life. Someone who God chose to be an instrument to bring people closer to Him. Oh, but I am. Because here I am, and I can say with confidence, I KNOW WHO GOD IS. Every one of those situations showed me a different side of God.

I know God is a provider. It hasn't always been about what I had in my bank account but about the God I serve who owns the cattle on a thousand hills. I know God is a mind-regulator when I was on the verge of losing my mind He stepped in. I know that He will be a father when daddy is gone; He comes into my room and wraps His loving arms around me even five year later the grief sneaks up on me and tries to consume me, but I know He is near the brokenhearted and saves the crushed in spirit. I've seen Him stop the very plans of man to do you harm and be my protector. I've heard people ask how is she making it when they did everything in their power to make me struggle. I've seen God keep His promises.

A.W. Tozer wrote, "What comes into our minds when we think about God is the most important thing about us."

We think it's our title on the job or at the church. We think it's the neighborhood we live in or who we are connected to. It's none of those things. It is what we believe about God that unlocks who God really wants to be in our lives.

Do you realize how much better your life would be if you started believing God? If God became more than a fictional character in your life. It's funny to me we believe God can save us, but we don't believe He can handle our daily lives, leading us, changing us, making us better. Every year I watch The Wizard of Oz. I'm sure you know the story. Dorothy went all the way to Oz, facing all kind of danger and uncertainty because she believed the wizard would get her back home. I think I was more disappointed than Dorothy when I first saw it and learned the wizard was just a phony behind a curtain. My God isn't though.

When my God says, He is able to do exceedingly abundantly MORE than we can ever ask or think. He has the authority to back it up. When my God say, I will supply all your needs according to His riches in glory. He means that. When my God says, "never will I leave you nor forsake you". That is not an empty promise. He's always right there. When he says, "When you pass through the waters, I will be with you; and through the rivers, they shall not overwhelm you; when you walk through fire you shall not be burned, and the flame shall not consume you." That promise is for you.

What else does my God say?

We are afflicted in every way, but not crushed; perplexed, but not driven to despair; persecuted, but not forsaken; struck down, but not destroyed; **II Corinthians 4:8** (Yet you walk around as if it's over for you and there is no more hope.)

"He gives strength to the weary and increases the power of the weak." **Isaiah 40:29** (Yet you walk around with a defeated attitude)

"If we confess our sins He is faithful and just to forgive us of our sins and cleanse us from all

unrighteousness." **I John 1:9** (Yet you walk around in bondage to something God has already forgiven you for that others may still be trying to hold over your head or you haven't forgiven yourself for.)

"Therefore, I tell you, whatever you ask in prayer, believe that you have received it, and it will be yours." **Mark 11:24** (Yet we walk around without, not just because we don't ask, but because we don't believe God can do it.)

What we believe about God

- **Shapes our actions**

- **Strengthens our right now**

- **Secures our future**

I am a big sports fan. And while I may live in Oklahoma City, home of the Thunder, I am a Los Angeles Lakers fan to my core. I bleed purple and gold. No not really. From the day of Kareem and Magic to the days of Kobe Bryant with and without Shaq or Pau Gasol and even now during the rebuilding phase. In addition to being a Laker fan I am a huge Michael Jordan fan. #23 is the epitome of greatness. I couldn't help but find myself cheering for the Bulls. One thing I was always aware of was the calmness of the coach and the calmness of his teammates. Phil Jackson, Scottie Pippin, and Dennis Rodman never worried because they knew who was on their team.

I still remember the 1997 playoff game 5 against the Utah Jazz when the series was tied 2-2. The Jazz felt they had everything working in their favor to snatch the advantage of the series, especially when they heard the rumor Jordan was ill. What they weren't ready for was the spirit that resided on the inside of Michael Jordan that said even in my illness I am going to play like a champion. And what happened Jordan ended the game with 38 points, seven rebounds, five assists, three steals, and a block helping to lead his team to a 3-2 lead and one step closer to their 5th championship.

There was another competition that happened one Friday night. The opponent thought everything was working in his favor. He watched them put the nails in his hands and feet, saw them pierce my Savior in the side, even watched when they took him off the cross and place him in a borrowed tomb. I'm sure the premature celebration started for Satan at that point, but He forgot whose team Jesus was on. He forgot the Scripture that said, "And I, if I be lifted up from the earth I'll draw all men unto me." He forgot what Jesus had said about the temple being destroyed but being rebuilt in three days. And there he was on Sunday morning with a loss instead of a victory.

Jesus is God's only begotten Son and He is our elder brother. We are afforded the promises of God through our relationship with Jesus Christ. God is our coach and He has given us the game plan for victory, yet we don't play like we are victorious. We play as though there is a chance we won't win. So, what you had a few failures in life. So, what you made a few mistakes. So, what the doctor said it's not looking good. So, what your husband wants to leave, or your wife doesn't love you anymore. So, what there's rumors of a layoff. So, what your finances are funny, and your family is fickle. So, what?

Who's on your team? It's time self-pity exits and enter blessed assurance. **Hebrews 10:22, 2 Timothy 1:12**

Exit discouragement and enter joyful expectation. **Romans 12:12; Psalm 71:14**

Exit defeat and enter guaranteed victory. **(Deut. 20:4; Psalm 60:12)**

Exit doubt and enter **Romans 8:28**. And we know? What do we know? All things work together for the good. For who? For them who love God and are the called according to His purpose.

My only question for you today is DO YOU BELIEVE? Do you believe to the point you are ready to say anything you ask of me, anywhere you want me to go? A place where your life truly reflects Not my will but thy will be done? A place where you can say like the psalmist in **Psalm 139**.

Where shall I go from your Spirit? Or where shall I flee from your presence? If I ascend to heaven, you are there! If I make my bed in Sheol, you are there! If I take the wings of the morning and dwell in the uttermost parts of the sea, even there your hand shall lead me, and your right hand shall hold me.

And you can say these words because you have come to not just know about God you Know God.

My prayer for you is that you become a Faith-Walker. You might not be like Enoch who because of His faith in God while living in a wicked world never died an earthly death, and just walked right on into Heaven. I do promise you your faith in God will be rewarded. For some it may be a spectacular reward, but for all we will receive the reward of life eternal in Heaven with God. You can and will make it in the valley.

Acknowledgements

Thank you, God! Even now with tears in my eyes I say with confidence "Blessed is she who believed the Lord would fulfill His promises to her."

Absolutely none of this would have been done without Him. Over fifteen years ago I began writing a book and every time a storm came, I quit. The original book was an autobiography of my life. I remember the day God stopped me in the middle of writing and said, "This is not the book I wanted you to write." Instead of glorifying God it was full of bitterness and anger. It wasn't until I was riding home one evening from work, praying a prayer of surrender to the Lord that He gave me the vision for the book you have just read.

After praying the song "For Every Mountain" started playing. God spoke and said, "That is the title for your book." I listened to the song and then He began speaking again. I turned on my recorder on the phone and recorded all eight principles. I went home, began writing, and the rest is history.

God, You are my everything. I am nothing without You. You have protected me and provided for me. You have corrected me in love. And most importantly, You have kept Your promise to never leave me nor forsake me. Most of my life I have felt like an outcast, never wanting to be different. However, I knew I was. I thank God for never giving up on me. I thank Him for choosing me to be a part of spreading the gospel. I thank God today because He is faithful.

I want to thank my parents, especially my mom, not just for taking me to church, but for teaching me at home. I thank them for requiring us to read our Bible every day and memorize Scripture. When I was young, the verses I memorized were only words. As I grew older, they became my foundation. They are the words I recite in the midnight hour, in my prayer closet, driving down the street, in silence in a crowded room. Thank you mama and thank you daddy.

I want to thank two very influential, praying women of God, Aunt Joyce "Bammie" Johnson and Sister Flora Gissandaner. These two ladies have supported and encouraged me in everything. They have prayed me out of some of the darkest times of my life. They are confidence keepers and awesome prayer warriors. I love them both with all my heart.

I would have never published one book without someone believing in me and seeing the hand of God on my life. Pastor A. G. Woodberry who gave me courage to stand even when I didn't think I was worthy or qualified. I taught my first Sunday School class under his leadership. Pastor Teron V. Gaddis who taught me how to focus solely on God and not look around me. Pastor G helped me to understand that there would be pain, everyone would not support you, but it will be worth it. My Godmother, Rev. Mona G. Rodgers, who cultivated spiritual boldness in me. My sisters, Monica, Veronica, Cynthia, Shenedra, and Marva Kookie. These ladies were my first best friends. We ride together through it all. My sisters in love, Staci and Kelli Woodberry who always believed in me and said to me that it was okay to lose people when my feelings were hurt. On any day, no matter what I am going through, I can call them or text them to pray for me and they do. They taught me that true friends are those who will pray for you and support your dreams.

God you are simply amazing. I stand on your Word that says, ***Beloved, we are God's children now, and what we will be has not yet appeared; but we know that when he appears we shall be***

like him, because we shall see him as he is. I
John 3:2

About the Author

Ramona Y. Simmons is a native of Oklahoma.
She serves in full-time ministry at Greater Bethel
Church in Oklahoma City, OK. She teaches in
both her district and state Congress of Christian
Education. She also recently launched her online
Bible study, Winning in the Word. She serves as
Chief of Staff for Pastor G Ministries. She is a
member of Alpha Kappa Alpha Sorority, Inc.
She is the proud mother of four wonderful
children, Khalil, Rachael, LaBraia, and Raven.
Her life verse is Acts 20:24. "But I do not
account my life of any value nor as precious to
myself, if only I may finish my course and the
ministry that I received from the Lord Jesus, to
testify to the gospel of the grace of God.

COMING SOON

TAKE A DEEPER DIVE INTO THE WORD OF GOD

Cultivate an attitude that declares, "No matter what I will trust God" with the 8-week Bible Study.

This study is for you if you desire to:

Create a life that welcomes God's sovereignty, releasing all control to Him.

Learn how not to give up by standing on solid biblical principles.

Endure through life's most difficult moments.

Accept that valleys are on the pathway to victory.